Emiratization in the UAE Labor Market

Georgia Daleure

Emiratization in the UAE Labor Market

Opportunities and Challenges

Springer

Georgia Daleure
Higher Colleges of Technology
Sharjah
United Arab Emirates

ISBN 978-981-10-2764-2 ISBN 978-981-10-2765-9 (eBook)
DOI 10.1007/978-981-10-2765-9

Library of Congress Control Number: 2016952884

Printed on acid-free paper

This Springer imprint is published by Springer Nature
The registered company is Springer Nature Singapore Pte Ltd.
The registered company address is: 152 Beach Road, #22-06/08 Gateway East, Singapore 189721, Singapore

In the name of Allah the beneficent and merciful. May the efforts spent in the preparation of this project reach its aim of promoting greater understanding and serving as a starting point for others seeking knowledge.

To my husband, Ahmad, and **ALL** *my dear children, for understanding my thirst for knowledge.*

To my father, William S. (Bill) Daleure, for all the sacrifices he has made so that his children, grandchildren, and great-grandchildren could achieve their dreams.

To my mother, Diana, for providing the love that only a mother can.

Preface

The United Arab Emirates (UAE) has become a well-known destination for celebrities, politicians, scholars, tourists, and others in recent years. Those who visit the UAE may enjoy the numerous and varied recreational facilities, participate in international sporting competitions, attend conferences or summit meetings, or engage in other regional and world-class events. The transformation of the social and physical infrastructure from nationalization in 1971 to the present serves as a success case in rapid modernization.

Most importantly, in a region filled with civil unrest and failing economies, the UAE remains politically stable and economically prosperous even through the global financial downturn in 2008. Therefore, it seems almost unbelievable that Emirati unemployment—specifically unemployment among young educated Emirati adults—has reached double digits in recent years. Concerns over rising Emirati unemployment in the early 2000s spurred the leadership of the country to initiate Emiratization policies, a type of "positive discrimination" that is characterized by some as detrimental to the country's continuing development.

To fully understand the complexities of Emirati unemployment and Emiratization, one must understand the creative and contributing factors through multiple lenses representing the perspectives of different stakeholders. This work attempts to describe the issues factually and impartially while presenting differing viewpoints when and where they exist. It is the differing viewpoints occurring simultaneously that make the issues interesting and worthy of an in-depth examination.

This work is particularly needed because in the scant amount of research available on Emirati unemployment, Emiratization, and the UAE labor market, the issues are explored mostly using a simple labor supply and demand model. Workers are viewed as one of the factors of production, and motivation for work is expressed in an equilibrium wage that balances the competitive desire of maximizing wages among workers with the desire of maximizing profit among the employers. This type of explanation, although valuable from one economic perspective, is not complete.

Some experts investigating the UAE labor market using the simplistic labor supply and demand framework attribute Emirati unemployment to Emirati preference for work in the saturated public sector due to the perception of more attractive compensation packages being offered in the public sector. Some experts attribute Emirati unemployment to an unwillingness among Emiratis to accept the wages being offered in the private sector that are pushed down by migrant workers willing to work for less than the Emirati reservation wage. Some of these experts even go so far as to suggest that it is the migrant workers that reside in the UAE who drive the UAE economy and replacing migrant workers with Emirati workers will decrease economic stability. This book presents the multiple, and sometimes contradicting, viewpoints that appear in academic literature and crop up in conversations of academics, policy makers, citizens, residents, and even casual observers of the UAE labor market.

Although studies do exist investigating the complexities of the UAE labor market, few experts have looked into the social, cultural, political, and environmental factors that affect the wage structure in the UAE labor market and the overall UAE economy. For example, studies are available examining the salary remittances of expatriate workers to their home countries. The great majority of studies mentioning remittance discuss the positive effects on the home countries of receiving remittances. However, the missing element is academic discourse on any negative effects of migrant worker remittances on the economies of the countries in which they work. Few experts have considered the long-term destabilizing effects of the unemployment, particularly young adult unemployment, on a minority citizenry in a country with a relatively high cost of living. As another example, few experts have calculated the employment costs and benefits of hiring Emiratis in the private sector aside from salaries. Few experts have factored in the cost of living differentials between Emirati and expatriate employees, i.e., economic expectations of each group, items on which salary is spent for each group, mentality of migrant versus indigenous worker, and so on. These aspects and others are examined in this book so that the reader has a rich and full picture of the factors leading to Emirati employment not just a cursory explanation of salaries and wages to understand the employment and unemployment of indigenous workers in the UAE. After all, it is only through sustainable employment of indigenous workers that a country can achieve and maintain a sustainable economy.

Every effort was made to include the most official and the most up-to-date sources, however, the story of the UAE was unfolding even as the last revision of this work was being finalized. In some cases, official documents mentioned on websites or in newspaper articles were available and referenced in the text. In other cases, the best available sources were newspaper articles or websites. In as many cases as possible, links to web documents, source articles, websites, and other sources are given in the reference section of each chapter. In addition, the online databases from which figures and statistics were obtained are mentioned in the chapters with the links provided so that readers may check facts and figures that were the best available but not necessarily up-to-date at the time of publication. The economic downturn of 2008 and subsequent drop in oil prices have drained the economies of the oil-producing countries prompting a decrease in spending in areas perceived to be expendable. As the economies have bounced back and stabilized, more funding has become available for scholarly activities. Therefore, it is anticipated that by the time this work proceeds through the production phase and becomes available to interested readers, updated and even more interesting data could be available.

Readers may query as to why so few Arabic sources are cited in this work when the official language of the country is Arabic. This is due to the multicultural nature of the working environment in the UAE in which most official documents, especially those intended for public release, are produced in a bilingual English–Arabic format. Official websites and web-based documents have both English and Arabic interfaces. When there was no substantive difference, I have used the English versions and cited the English versions since this work is produced in English.

Providing good quality bilingual documents is possible in a large part because UAE nationals overwhelmingly choose to study in federally funded postsecondary institutions which use English as the medium of instruction. Therefore, most of the government employees who have postsecondary degrees are proficient in both English and Arabic, and many government employees are multilingual, possessing a working proficiency in regional languages such as Hindi, Ordu, or Farsi. The UAE prides itself on having educated its citizens to be bilingual and on producing materials that are usable at the international level.

The book is organized into 10 interrelated chapters. Chapter 1 serves as an introduction to sustainable employment in the UAE. Chapter 2 describes the transition of the UAE economy from a traditional economy to the present modern economy mentioning some of the challenges affecting the UAE economy and labor market. Chapter 2 gives an overview of the modern-day UAE emphasizing the international attention that the UAE has received from its diversification efforts. Chapter 3 presents the economic vision for the UAE and provides a brief overview of the economic environments of each of the seven emirates focusing on diversification strategies implemented in each one. Chapter 4 describes the UAE economy in depth along with underlying factors contributing to Emirati unemployment. Chapter 5 highlights the roles and contributions of women in Emirati society emphasizing the encouragement given by the government to Emirati women to obtain higher education and work outside the home if they wish to do so. Chapter 6 focuses on salaries in the UAE and breaks down salaries by nationality, industry, occupation, education level, age, location, sector, and gender to show how general mean salary figures can mask vast disparities between high salaries and low salaries. Chapter 7 examines the role of migrant workers in general and explains the effects of formal and informal salary remittances on the UAE economy. Chapter 8 relates ways in which social transitions may have contributed to Emirati unemployment, especially among young Emirati adults. Chapter 9 focuses on the development of education in the UAE with emphasis on ways in which education can bolster employment or impede it. Chapter 10 summarizes the main points of the work and puts forth the dichotomy of sustainability versus complementarity of labor in the UAE.

Multiple conclusions may be drawn based on the information presented due to the complexity of the concepts, multiple perspectives of analysis, and varied viewpoints of stakeholder. However, the author leaves the conclusions to the reader, and focuses on promoting understanding by giving rich sophisticated descriptions and accurate explanations of the factors surrounding Emirati unemployment and Emiratization efforts in the UAE labor market. It is hoped that this work will be a useful starting point for those interested in conducting further research on Emiratization, the UAE labor market, and other related topics.

Finally, I would like to acknowledge the exceptional efforts of the professionals who reviewed all or parts of the manuscript of this book to assure that it represents the views of a broad range of stakeholders. The reviewers include an economist, a specialist in Middle East history, educators, and experts in the UAE business environment. Some of the reviewers are Emiratis and all of the reviewers lived and worked in the UAE during this time of phenomenal transition. For their magnificent efforts, I would like to thank Dr. Zain Hassan Al Shareef, Mr. Timothy White, Mr. Ali Khalifa Al Suwaidi, Dr. Patrick Kane, and Ms. Parminder Gill.

Sharjah, United Arab Emirates Georgia Daleure

Contents

Chapter 1
Introduction to Sustainable Employment

Abstract Rapid economic development and prosperity elevated the living standards of Emiratis and raised the profile of the country to an internationally competitive level. While enabling economic benefits, rapid development has been linked to domestic concerns that are being addressed by the country's leadership in creative and innovative ways. Sustainable employment of country's citizens is one such concern. As expatriate business people and workers flocked to the UAE to take advantage of the economic opportunities, a population imbalance occurred in which citizens of the UAE became the citizen minority. Even with abundant employment opportunities in its vibrant private sector and a minority citizen population representing less than 20 % of the total population, several interrelated factors serve as challenges to full Emirati employment, especially among young Emirati adults. This chapter discusses the relationship between socioeconomic development and unemployment among Emiratis, especially among educated young Emirati adults. The chapter concludes by describing Emiratization and explaining the role of Emiratization as a catalyst for sustainable Emirati employment.

Keywords United arab emirates (UAE) · Emirati unemployment · UAE labor market · Emiratization

1.1 Introduction

The United Arab Emirates (UAE) emerged into the global marketplace in the last few decades of the twentieth century. Rapid economic development enabled the UAE to transition in less than half a century from a mostly rural agricultural society to an urbanized society with a lifestyle on par with other modernized nations of the world (Shiliro 2013).

While enabling economic benefits, rapid development has been linked to domestic concerns that are being addressed by the country's leadership in creative and innovative ways. Sustainable employment of the country's citizens is one such concern, the discussion of which is the core purpose of this work. This chapter serves as the

G. Daleure, *Emiratization in the UAE Labor Market*,
DOI 10.1007/978-981-10-2765-9_1

starting point by explaining the relationship between socioeconomic development and unemployment among Emiratis, especially among educated young Emirati adults. The chapter concludes by describing Emiratization and explaining the role of Emiratization as a catalyst for sustainable Emirati employment. The topics introduced briefly in chapter one are expanded upon in the consecutive chapters.

1.2 Effects of Socioeconomic Shifts on the UAE Labor Market

Rapid economic development and prosperity elevated the living standards of Emiratis and raised the profile of the country to an internationally competitive level. As expatriate business people and workers flocked to the UAE to take advantage of the economic opportunities, a population imbalance occurred in which citizens of the UAE became the minority.

According to the Abu Dhabi-based Arab Monetary Fund, the population growth rate of the UAE remained steady at over 5 % annually from 1983 to 1995, the highest in the Arab region. The report states that the factors contributing to the sustained population growth rate include an increase in the Emirati population mostly due to decreasing child mortality, generally better health services and growing numbers of expatriates gaining employment in the country (Kalwach 2003). Experts on human resource management in the Middle East including Budhwar and Mellahi (2007) suggest that the rapid rise of expatriates residing in the country—with their differing values, beliefs, customs, and languages—sparked demographic transitions in the country resulting in social, cultural, and economic consequences.

The imbalance grew so steeply that by 2012 Emiratis comprised less than 20 % (about 1.8 million people) of the country's estimated total population of about 8.2 million people and only about 10 % of the total workforce in the UAE (World Bank 2014). Although overall Emirati unemployment remained steady at about 4 % from 2005 to 2012, Emirati young adult unemployment rose steadily from 7.8 % in 2005 to nearly 12 % over the same period (United Arab Emirates 2014). Another source reported Emirati young adult unemployment as being closer to 14 % in 2012 creating concern because more than half (51 % in 2012) of the Emirati population was under the age of 18 at that time (Sherif 2013). The concerns of policy makers increased as growing numbers of fresh Emirati graduates, many of whom with postsecondary degrees, entered into the labor market and did not find suitable employment.

Relatively high unemployment among young Emirati adults reflects the dual realities that exist in the UAE labor market which may disadvantage Emirati job seekers. According to some labor market experts, young Emirati adults, even those with postsecondary degrees, face stiff competition for suitable jobs in the private sector (Toledo 2013; Forstenlechner and Rutledge 2011). The expatriates competing for suitable jobs often possess even more advanced degrees and more work experience than the young Emirati adult job seekers. In addition, the expatriate employees tend to be willing to work for a lower wage than Emirati job seekers or may be willing to endure working conditions that are unacceptable to Emiratis.

The second important reality, as demonstrated Chap. 6, is that only about 20–30 % of the jobs available in the private sector are knowledge economy jobs for which young Emirati adults are being prepared. Supporting this assertion, in 2013, it was estimated that Emiratis occupied less than 1 % of the over 4 million jobs available in the private sector (AlShaiba 2014). Studies conducted around that time revealed that more Emiratis were likely to enter the private sector workforce if workplace environments were made more attractive to Emirati employees by increasing cultural sensitivity in the workplace (Al Shareef and Daleure 2011; Daleure 2012). Other studies recommended that freeing up the movement of expatriate employees already working in the country, i.e., making it easier for expatriate employees to change jobs, would have an overall positive affect on Emirati employment (Forstenlechner and Rutledge 2011; Rutledge et al. 2011; Toledo 2013).

In late 2013, the UAE Ministry of Human Resources and Emiratization (MHRE), previously known as the UAE Ministry of Labor (MOE), called upon the private sector to create between 10,000 and 20,000 new jobs annually to absorb unemployed Emiratis between the ages of 15 and 60 years old (Kapur 2013). New labor policies accompanied the call signaling a shift toward more flexibility in the labor market. The new policies allowed expatriate employees, upon completion of their notice period, to change employers without needing to get permission from their original employers. Other new policies authorized part-time employment for Emiratis wishing to work part-time and paved the way for employment opportunities for expatriates in the country on a spousal or parent visa (D'Souza 2012; Kapur 2014).

The opportunities established by the new policies provided expanded employment options for Emirati youth seeking work experience, Emirati women entering the workforce for the first time later in life, and Emiratis of both genders seeking to further their careers outside the saturated public sector (Daleure and Al Shareef 2015). Allowing expatriates on spousal and parental visa to work enabled private sector employers to reduce labor costs on jobs that were not attractive to Emiratis so that Emiratis could be hired in more desirable positions at attractive wages.

1.3 Sustainable Economic Development with Emiratization as the Catalyst

It seems illogical that a country could have double digit unemployment of young adult citizens, many of whom are graduates of postsecondary institutions, when the country has abundant employment opportunities available in the vibrant private sector, wealth generated by oil revenues used to fund major public works and infrastructure development, and a citizen population that constitutes less than one-fifth of the total population (Schiliro 2013). However, the rate of economic growth has outpaced the needed transitions of both the collective Emirati mindset favoring public sector employment, discussed in more detail in the Chap. 8, and the perceptions of some private sector employers who perceive hiring citizens as being more costly than hiring expatriates, discussed in more detail in Chap. 10. Experts and policy makers who perceive Emirati unemployment as a side-effect of rapid development, expect that Emirati unemployment will decrease as the collective Emirati mindset and the private sector employer perceptions adjust to the reality of current and future global economic conditions.

In an effort to jump-start the integration of Emiratis into the workforce, increase the awareness of benefits of working in the private sector among Emirati job seekers, and expose private sector employers to the benefits of employing indigenous workers, the leadership of the country enacted labor laws and nationalization policies that prioritize hiring Emiratis, a process called Emiratization (Abu Dhabi Emiratization Forum 2010). As a form of positive discrimination, Emiratization policies provide incentives to organizations and corporations that hire UAE nationals and administer penalties to those who avoid hiring UAE nationals (Toledo 2013). Emiratization efforts are seen by some as a positive way to catalyze the integration of UAE nationals into the workforce and by others as a placebo masking long-term productivity-based integration of Emiratis into the workforce (AlWaqfi and Forstenlechner 2014; Emirati health 2016; Ministry mandates 2016).

Up to early 2016, Emiratization efforts have had limited success, perhaps because they have not sufficiently addressed the holistic elements contributing to the issues surrounding Emirati unemployment (Schiliro 2013). However, in 2016 the policy makers augmented their efforts, described in more detail in Chaps. 9 and 10, by enacting four major ministerial restructures, enabling Emiratization policies to reach further into the relatively untapped private sector areas, and by establishing the *Ministry of Happiness* to assure that the needs of all, residents and citizens of the UAE, are considered when making important decisions about the country's future (UAE cabinet 2016).

This work discusses issues related to employment of UAE nationals—particularly educated young Emirati adults—from the framework of holistic sustainable development which integrates the economic, environmental, historical, social, cultural, and political dimensions to get a more comprehensive picture of the challenges facing indigenous workers. It is hoped that the ideas provided in this work will serve as a background upon which new studies can by developed and will assist policy makers to continue to enhance the UAE labor market.

References

Abu Dhabi Emiratization Forum: Improving retention by harnessing motivation. (2010, May 30). *Report of key findings*. Abu Dhabi: Abu Dhabi University.

AlShaiba, A. (2014). *Key perspectives on preparing UAE nationals for employment. In the future of eduation in the UAE: Innovation and knowledge production* (pp. 67–95). Abu Dhabi: The Emirates Center for Strategic Studies and Research (ECSSR).

Al Shareef, Z., & Daleure, G. (2011). *Exploring UAE national competitiveness to promote overall economic sustainability: Achievements and challenges*. Paper presented at Counselling Arabia International 2011: Youth at the Crossroads Conference in Sharjah, UAE. Available at https://www.academia.edu/6662557/Exploring_UAE_National_Competitiveness_to_Promote_Overall_Economic_Sustainabilty_Achievements_and_Challenges

AlWaqfi, M. A., & Forstenlechner, I. (2014). Barriers to Emiratization: The role of policy design and institutional environment in determining the effectiveness of Emiratization. *The International Journal of Human Resource Management, 25*(2), 167–189. doi:10.1080/09585192.2013.826913.

Budhwar, P., & Mellahi, K. (2007). Introduction: Human resource management in the Middle East. *International Journal of Human Resource Management, 18*(1), 2–10.

Daleure, G. (2012, December). *From vision to reality: The road to full employment of Emiratis in the economy of the United Arab Emirates*. Paper Presented at the 1st Annual Human Capital and Sustainable Development Conference, December 12–14, 2012. Sharjah, UAE: Human Resources Department.

Daleure, G., & Al Shareef, Z. (2015). Exploring under-representation of young Emirati adults in the UAE private sector by examining Emirati job Satisfaction. *Working Paper No. 9*. Ras Al Khaimah: Sheikh Saud Bin Saqr Al Qasimi Foundation for Policy Research.

D'Souza, C. (2012, January 31). New policy allows Emiratis to take on part-time jobs. *The Gulf News Newspaper* Online. Available at http://gulfnews.com/business/sectors/employment/new-policy-allows-emiratis-to-take-on-part-time-jobs-1.973809

Emirati health and safety officers 'must be employed in construction sector'. (2016, July 16). *The National Newspaper* Online. Available at http://www.thenational.ae/uae/government/emirati-health-and-safety-officers-must-be-employed-in-construction-sector

Forstenlechner, I., & Rutledge, E. J. (2011). The GCC's "Demographic Imbalance": Perceptions, realities and policy options. *Middle East Policy, 18*(4), 25–43.

Kalwach, N. (2003, June 12). The UAE has highest population growth rate in the Arab World. *Gulf News Newspaper* Online. Available at http://gulfnews.com/news/uae/general/uae-has-highest-population-growth-rate-in-arab-world-1.358637

Kapur, S. (2013, October 23). Private sector jobs alert: Emiratis now more open to joining. *Emirates 24/7 Newspaper Online*. Available at: http://www.emirates247.com/news/emirates/private-sector-jobs-alert-Emiratis-now-more-open-to-joining

Kapur, S. (2014, October 30). Revealed: Who can and can't work part-time at another job in UAE. *Emirates 24/7 Newspaper Online*. Available at http://www.emirates247.com/news/emirates/revealed-who-can-and-can-t-work-part-time-at-another-job-in-uae-2014-10-30-1.568184

Ministry mandates companies to employ Emiratis in data-entry positions. (2016, July 20). *The National Newspaper* Online. Available at http://www.thenational.ae/uae/government/ministry-mandates-companies-to-employ-emiratis-in-data-entry-positions

Rutledge, E. J., Al Shamsi, F., Bassioni, Y., & Al Sheikh, H. (2011). Women, labour market nationalisation policies and human resource development in the Arab Gulf States. *Human Resource Development International, 14*(2), 183–193.

Schiliro, D. (2013, Summer). Diversification and development of the United Arab Emirates' economy. *Journal of Applied Economic Sciences*, 228–239.

Sherif, S. (2013). Macroeconomic policy, localization, and reducing unemployment: The crucial human resource issues for the UAE. *Competitiveness Review: An International Business Journal, 23*(2), 158–174.

Toledo, H. (2013). The political economy of Emiratization in the UAE. *Journal of Economic*.

UAE Cabinet approves national charter for happiness. (2016, March 20). *Gulf News Newspaper Online*. Available at http://gulfnews.com/news/uae/environment/uae-cabinet-approves-national-charter-for-happiness-1.1694177

United Arab Emirates economic data. (2014, July 4). *Quandl*. Retrieved from http://www.quandl.com/uae/uae-economy-data

World Bank. (2014, June 25). Retrieved from http://data.worldbank.org/country/united-arab-emirates

Chapter 2
UAE Goes Global

Abstract The inhabitants of the area now known as the UAE were successful business people, trades people, and administrators well-connected with their regional counterparts, long before the discovery of oil. The UAE transitioned from a traditional economy to the modern global economy in less than half a century, however, the rapid economic growth brought about socio-economic shifts including a demographic imbalance in which UAE nationals comprise less than 20 % of the total population and only about 10 % of the workforce. Diversification efforts were instituted from the early days of nationalization to allow the country to maintain a prosperous economy even after the oil revenues stop flowing. Federally funded public works and extensive infrastructure development provided the elements needed to create a safe and attractive work and living environment that attracts business people, tourists, and expatriate employees from counties around the globe. Film crews have used the UAE as backdrop for well-known productions. Sporting events, concerts, art shows, and other entertainment are held in world class venues around the country in addition to educational conferences, seminars, and training courses. Foreign investment-friendly economic policies combined with the establishment of free-zone areas have encouraged multinational companies of all sizes to set up regional hubs or headquarters in the UAE. Even though the UAE faces challenges, in a troubled region surrounded by counties experiencing economic turmoil and issues related to uneven distribution of wealth, the UAE stands as example of openness and prosperity.

Keywords United Arab Emirates (UAE) unemployment · UAE labor market

2.1 The Transition from a Traditional Economy to a Global Economy

Rapid economic and social progress in the UAE cannot be attributed solely to the discovery of oil. There are numerous examples of oil exporting countries that have not achieved a similar level of modernization and social progress. The inhabitants

G. Daleure, *Emiratization in the UAE Labor Market*,
DOI 10.1007/978-981-10-2765-9_2

of the area now known as the UAE were successful business people, trades people, and administrators, well connected with their regional counterparts, long before the discovery of oil. This chapter describes the transition from a traditional economy to the modern global economy that the UAE has become and points out opportunities and challenges associated with the transition.

2.1.1 Overview of Pre-oil Society

From the early years of the nation, the leadership of the UAE had a vision of using the oil proceeds to upgrade the economy and improve the lifestyle of the people and is clearly spelled out in the *UAE Vision 2021* document (Government of UAE 2010b). The method for achieving success was by *upgrading and modernizing* the familiar economic practices previously followed for thousands of years. The familiar process consisted of anchoring the economy on one main economic product, natural pearls in the pre-oil days, then using the proceeds to support ancillary industries and promote trade. Proceeds from the main economic product and trade were then used by the leadership to drive public works and establish social services. For thousands of years, natural pearls were seasonally harvested and served as the backbone of the regional economy. The pearl industry supported active trading bases and promoted contact with other regional trading partners. These practices were a part of the economic and cultural fabric of the region mentioned in century's old written texts and practiced until the natural pearl market collapsed in the early 1930s (Davidson 2005; Smith 2008).

The inhabitants of the region devised ingenious ways to maximize the other meager resources available to them in the arid and inhospitable desert environment. Inhabitants of the region adapted to the lack of rainfall in the desert climate by utilizing underground water sources obtained from wells. Underground water was transported to settlement areas inland and near the coast and to agricultural areas in sophisticated irrigation systems known as *wadis*. Oasis areas provided with irrigated underground water were able to produce seasonal fruits, vegetables, and grains. Securing and transporting water from underground sources enabled continuous inhabitation of the region for millenia even though the UAE has no naturally occurring surface water (Magee 2014; Sherif et al. 2012).

Surviving in adversity using the natural resources at hand is an attribute for which the inhabitants of the region were well known (Al-Sayegh 1998). Dates were used as a food source well suited as sustenance for overland travelers or as a dietary supplement for seafarers. The palm fronds were used as construction material for houses, ropes, and other household items. The main dietary staple came from the abundant fish and sea life along the coast. Animals such as camels, goats and sheep were used for meat and milk. Although camels were used for milk and sometimes for food, they were most importantly used for transport in the harsh desert environment. The inhabitants of the region were for the most part self-sufficient and used the revenues from pearling and trade to purchase items such as textiles and rice that they could not produce locally themselves (Magee 2014; Potts 2001).

The contributions of women in the traditional society were well acknowledged with women empowered to run families when men were frequently away traveling for trading purposes or off-shore during pearling season (El-Saadi 2012; Heard-Bey 2001; Sonbol 2012). It is not surprising that the leadership of the country integrated women fully in the development process by making education of both genders mandatory up to 10th grade, by establishing post-secondary institutions specifically for Emirati women, and by legally empowering women to work outside the home (Al-Sayegh 2001; Government of the UAE 2010b).

Throughout the history of the region tribal rulers collected a share of the revenues from pearling, fishing, trading, and other economic activities, exemplifying an early form of rent-gathering. In exchange, they provided protection and administrative services for their constituencies (Al-Sayegh 1998). Experience with the early forms of rent-gathering and administration provided the training and expertise needed for negotiating interests and managing the economic and social transitions that occurred after the discovery of oil. For these reasons and others, the area now known as the UAE has been a prosperous area, continuously inhabited for thousands of years, and well connected with the other civilizations in the region (Jasim 2012; Mansour 2013). With a bit of modernization and upgrading, the same attributes that contributed to the historic success of the region also enabled the country to achieve economic success in modern times.

2.1.2 Pre-oil Era Economics

The debilitating poverty experienced by inhabitants of the region in the pre-oil era, often written about by Western observers, was caused by a combination of factors. The economy suffered from the isolation that was imposed on the region while under protectorate status during the colonial period and the collapse of the natural pearl market. The indigenous people of the Trucial States, the name of the area now known as the UAE during protectorate era, were not allowed venture off-shore except for fishing and pearling without special permission from the protectorate government. In addition, the only permitted trading partners were the British East India Company and other approved companies, often to the detriment of their indigenous trading partners (Al-Qasimi 1988). The inhabitants of the Trucial States had no choice but to continue to practice their century's old traditional economic pursuit of pearling in isolation while the rest of the world experienced the industrial revolution and progressive modernization. With the economy so heavily dependent on one product, the collapse of the natural pearl market started the economic downturn that was exacerbated by the worldwide economic ramifications of the Great Depression and Second World War. The combined effects were devastating to the region, wiping out the fortunes and progress of previous generations (Al-Fahim 1995). A small amount of relief came when some of Trucial States rulers received concessions for air landing rights and oil exploration rights from their protectorate governors (Al-Qasimi 2012). The modest new rentier wealth enabled Trucial States rulers to initiate a few public improvement projects aimed at upgrading the living standards of their people (Davidson 2005).

2.1.3 Nationalization Without Fanfare or Celebrations

In the days prior to unification, some experts seemed to doubt that the UAE could stand on its own, let alone prosper. In 1966, a few years before the British announced their plans to withdraw from the region, David Holden, an iconic Middle East news correspondent expressed his opinion that "there is no realistic possibility of the present Gulf rulers coming together of their own accord in any political group worth mentioning" (quoted in Davidson 2005, p. 48). Despite the seeming lack of confidence of some observers, when the withdrawal announcement was made in 1968, the rulers of the individual Trucial States led by the Shaikh Zayed Al-Nahyan, Ruler of Abu Dhabi, and Shaikh Rashid Al-Maktoum, Ruler of Dubai, united. The federation was signed into existence on December 2, 1971.

The process of nationalization occurred in the UAE with little attention from the rest of the world. Geoffrey Arthur, the British political resident present at the time of nationalization, remarked, "I do not recollect that a single special correspondent of a major Western newspaper, let alone a politician or statesman, took the trouble to attend the ceremony of its formation" (quoted in Davidson 2005, p. 49). Elderly citizens, interviewed for a study about life in the UAE before and during nationalization, indicated that even though they heard about nationalization efforts at the time by word of mouth or on the radio, they did not fully appreciate the significance of the event until much later (Abdulrahman 2013).

Although outwardly supportive, even the UAE's partner in oil production expressed skepticism retrospectively. In a report released in 1977, the Undersecretary for Political Affairs of the United States of America, Joseph Sisco, admitted to a senate committee that "the United States had also expressed grave doubts about the UAE holding together back in 1971" (quoted in Davidson 2005, p. 49). Yet, despite skepticism on numerous fronts, the leadership set out to establish a nation that was uniquely Arab and Islamic and, at the same time, modern and integrated into the fabric of the global society (Ahmad et al. 2011).

2.1.4 Economic Growth Commences

After an economically stifling period of colonial isolation from the early 1800s to the mid-1900s, the British withdrew and country nationalized, around the same time that oil revenues began to flow (Heard-Bey 2005). The leadership used the new source of income to initiate massive public projects to start developing the physical and social infrastructure of the country from the ground up. Roads were built, residential areas were developed, market areas were improved, communications systems were established, and the basic infrastructure was put into place to provide health care, education, other much needed social services (Al-Sayegh 1998). At the same time, policies and procedures from around the globe were studied and used in the development of the modern laws and legal system that now exist in the country (Rugh 2010).

The leadership effectively recalibrated the traditional economy by swapping out natural pearls, a product highly valued in the premodern global economy, for oil, a product highly valued in the modern world economy craving energy. Oil revenue was used to fund the major modernization efforts that facilitated trade and attracted international companies seeking to establish a presence in the MENA and GCC regions. Another part of the re-calibration included re-conceptualizing the tribal social structure using the notion of citizenship as a way to incorporate all Emiratis into one cohesive supersized extended family, a super tribe, with all receiving a share of the membership benefits (Heard-Bey 2005). Realizing the finite nature of oil as a main economic anchor and retaining vivid memories of the repercussions that followed the collapse of the natural pearl industry, the founding fathers of the country advocated diversification of the economy from the early stages of nationalization (Augustine 2014; Shuey 2016).

In forming the country, the leaders of the individual emirates consolidated their collective authorities to form a central government with specific powers including administration, protection, and managing natural resources assigned to it. The main ruling body of the federal government, the Supreme Council, included representation from all of the seven emirates. All powers not specifically delegated to the federal government were retained by the leaders of the individual emirates. The federal government prioritized upgrading the physical and social infrastructure needed to stimulate the national economy and sub-economies of each of the individual emirates and upgrade the quality of life for its constituents (Herb 1999).

During the massive growth and modernization phase, foreign labor was urgently needed at every skill and education level (Malit and AlYouha 2013). In the meantime, the leadership invested heavily in its most precious resource, the education of its people which is discussed later in more detail in Chaps. 8 and 9 (Heard-Bey 2001). The leadership of the country envisioned that as skilled Emiratis emerged from the newly established educational system, the educated Emiratis would be prioritized for employment, to contribute their skills and efforts to support the nation that provided them with so much, naturally decreasing the overall dependency on foreign labor (Government of the UAE 2016).

2.1.5 *Preparing for a UAE Without Oil*

Economic policies were put into place vigorously promoting an economic shift away from oil as the main GDP contributor (Al-Sadafy 2010). The goal was to move toward a service-based knowledge economy with technology enabling productivity gains reducing the number of workers needed to sustain an acceptable GDP. At the same time, the economic diversification aimed at creating new jobs that would be attractive to nationals (Government of UAE 2010b). Preparations *for the day when the last barrel of oil is shipped from its shores* were announced by H. H. Sheikh Mohammed bin Rashid Al Maktoum, Prime Minister and Vice President of the UAE after a retreat during which policy makers met to consider the economic future of the country (Shuey 2016). Discussed at the retreat were the sweeping restructuring efforts that were enacted to enable the UAE to better achieve its social and economic goals. The official UAE government website states that:

> The UAE Federal Government is under the process of major structural changes. Several federal ministries, authorities and institutions are being ceased or merged. H. H. Sheikh Mohammed bin Rashid Al Maktoum, Prime Minister and Vice President of the UAE and Ruler of Dubai announced these changes on 8 February 2016 through his official Twitter account as part of the three-day World Government Summit… In the new government strategy, the UAE will have a roadmap to outsource most government services to the private sector. (Government of the Future, n.d).

To improve government efficiency and enhance the efforts of Emiratization, structural changes have been applied to four ministries including the Ministry of Labor, renamed as the Ministry of Human Resources and Emiratization (MoHRE). The name change highlights the Ministry's continuous concern for all human resources in the country and emphasizes the special focus on Emiratization by dedicating a subsection to providing training and development opportunities for UAE national employees. Two recent decrees exemplify the MoHRE's commitment to Emiratization in the private sector by mandating that:

- all companies with 1000 or more employees employ Emiratis in data entry positions and
- all construction companies with 500 or more employees employ Emirati Health and Safety officers (Emirati Health 2016; Ministry mandates 2016).

2.1.6 Emiratization and Privatization as the Way Forward

Emiratization and privatization, according to the leadership of the UAE, are both needed as part of the overall labor market correction that must take place to create a sustainable economy. As stated on the UAE official website, many of the heavily subsidized public sector jobs will be privatized, thereby contributing to creating new jobs in the private sector. By assisting in the creation of desirable jobs through privatization, the UAE government hopes to aid in transitioning the collective social mindset away from preference for public sector jobs. It is further anticipated that dependence on foreign labor can be decreased by making progress toward establishing a knowledge-based economy with the desirable jobscreated being filled by the increasing the indigenous population (AlWasmi 2014; Malit and AlYouha 2013).

Experts, including Behery (2009), explain that as the social and economic transitions more fully align with the emerging social and economic realities, Emirati unemployment rates will decrease because Emiratis will find more jobs that suit their skills and abilities at an acceptable salary. Oil revenues provided the means to rapidly modernize the physical infrastructure of the country in less than the lifetime of a person, but transitioning the collective social mindset and re-aligning private sector employment practices are proving to be longer and more complex processes.

2.2 Progress from Diversification Efforts

The *World Fact Book* (United Arab Emirates 2014) ranked the UAE as the sixth largest oil producing country in 2014 by virtue of exporting over 2.7 million barrels of oil daily. The only GCC country to top the UAE in 2014 was Saudi Arabia with over 6.8 million barrels of oil exported daily (Katzman 2010). The massive public projects and continual infrastructure upgrades funded by the oil revenues allowed the leadership to modernize the country and create an attractive business environment. To further invigorate private sector growth, the leadership of UAE established trade policies favorable to foreign investment including re-exporting and other private sector enterprises. The diversification strategy aimed at diversification at a federal level by providing the tools for diversification at the individual emirate level. Because the seven emirates vary widely in population density, geographic features, and available natural resources, the diversification strategy empowers the individual emirates to expand their own local economy utilizing their own strengths and resources to increase individual contributions to the GDP. At the same time, citizens in all seven emirates enjoy similar access to social and civil services provided by the federal government regardless of the GDP contribution of the emirate in which they live.

According to a recently released Standard and Poor's report, the diversification efforts seem to be working. The report states that "although the UAE remains highly oil dependent, it is the least vulnerable to oil price declines or export volume declines among the six GCC countries" having lowered its overall national dependence on oil exports by 15 % from 2001 to 2013 (Augustine 2014). In 2005 revenue from oil exports reportedly made up about three fourths (73 %) of the nation's GDP while more recent reports place oil exports at approximately 25 % of the overall GDP (Government of UAE 2016).

Presently, the emirates of Abu Dhabi and Dubai contribute the most revenue toward the GDP with approximately 60 % coming from the emirate of Abu Dhabi which contains the capital city and has the largest oil reserves. Dubai contributes around 29 % of the GDP with most revenues coming from the non-petroleum-related sectors including construction, manufacturing, trade, real estate, transport, storage and communication, and finance (Istaitieh et al. 2007). Chapter 3 examines the sub-economies of the seven emirates in more detail.

2.3 Surviving the Global Economic Crisis and Falling Oil Prices

The effects of global financial crisis in 2008 were felt around the world and, for some countries in the region, profoundly. However, the economy of the UAE was able to weather the storm by utilizing an economic cushion to absorb the most devastating effects of the crisis and minimize the negative impact on the economy. A summary of the effects of the global financial crisis is available in the *Analytical Report on Economic and Social Dimensions in the United Arab Emirates* (Government of the UAE 2010a). The report explains that in 2009, the UAE government

> intervened through aggressive expansionary monetary and fiscal policies to cushion the adverse effects of the global slowdown by adopting counter-cyclical stabilization policies to generate aggregate demand and ensure that the banking system has enough liquidity to finance the economic recovery (Government of UAE 2010a, p. 10).

The report goes on to state that even with the liquidity policies in place, the global financial crisis took its toll on the real estate sector in Dubai. However, investments in projects such as the Dubai Metro, Burj Khalifa, and soft infrastructure enhancements such as the e-gov services initiatives have created efficiencies that offset the real estate sector setbacks.

The declining price of oil in the global marketplace continues to serve as a major challenge to economic growth in the UAE. During the crisis period, oil prices dropped drastically from 2008 to 2009 as shown in Table 2.1.

Oil prices rose to an all-time high in 2012 then plummeted to the lowest prices in more than a decade in early 2016. Later in 2016 the price of oil gradually began to rise.

With oil as a main economic product, the plummeting oil prices affected the GDP growth rates through the crisis period. Table 2.2 shows the transition in GDP growth rates in the UAE context as compared to the global context revealing that although the growth rates slowed considerably, the economy did not go into decline.

Table 2.1 Oil prices from 2002 to June 2016 (Statistica 2016; Oil-Price.net 2016)

Date	Price of oil/per barrel US$	Date	Price of oil/per barrel US$
2002	24.36	2010	77.38
2003	28.10	2011	107.46
2004	36.05	2012	109.40
2005	50.59	2013	105.87
2006	61.00	2014	96.29
2007	69.04	2015	49.49
2008	94.10	2016	27.63
2009	60.86	June 2016	48.00

Table 2.2 Global GDP growth during through global financial crisis (Government of UAE 2010a)

Year	Global GDP growth (%)	GDP growth in the UAE (%)
2007	5.5	11.1
2008	3.2	12.3
2009	−2.2	1.6

As shown in this subsection, the UAE faced financial challenges and pulled through by enacting policies designed to strengthen and interconnect the interests of the individual emirates.

2.4 Population Growth and Composition

Population numbers in the region have been affected by the economic status of the region as business people and migrant workers arrived to take part in economic prosperity and departed in times of economic hardship. Table 2.3 illustrates population growth and declines from the beginning of the twentieth century to the present.

The large number of migrant workers who immigrated to the UAE during the prosperous period of the pearling heyday are reflected in the estimated population figure for 1904. Following the collapse of the natural pearl market, many of the expatriate merchants and businesspeople returned back to their countries of origin. The population did not recover even half a century later in the population estimate just after the Second World War in 1950. The population decline in 1950 reflects not only the decrease in expatriate workers but also the high mortality rate of indigenous people mainly due to impoverishment and lack of modern healthcare and social services available at the time (Al-Fahim 1995; Al-Sayegh 2001).

Table 2.3 Population growth from the early 1900s to present (Kawach 2003; Macris 2015; Government of UAE 2011; UAE Population 1960–2016 2016)

Year	Estimated population
1904	80,000
1950	70,000
1968*	80,000
1970	232,000
1975	557,887
1985	1,379,303
1995	2,411,041
2005*	4,106,427
2010	8,264,070
2014	9,400,000

*1968 and 2005 are census figures not estimates

In the late 1960s, news of the economic opportunities in the early days of the oil era began to spread. Around the same time, the British lifted travel restrictions as they announced their 3 year plan to withdraw from the region beginning in 1968. As shown in Table 2.3, a massive population swell occurred with the population nearly tripling in the few years prior to nationalization. Rapid increases in population during the oil boom of the 1970s and the early 1980s occurred as mostly Arab expatriate workers migrated to the UAE, providing a timely and effective way of addressing the massive labor needs arising from rapid development (Yousef 2005).

In the early 1980s migrant workers from the Indian subcontinent arrived in increasing numbers, many of whom were willing to work for less compensation than their Arab counterparts (Weiner 1982). From the 1990s, the economy increased steadily through two Gulf Wars, declining oil revenues, and even through the Global Financial Crisis in the mid-2000s. The population roughly doubled every 5 years from 1970 to 2010 as shown in Table 2.3.

As the economy expanded in the late 1980s and early 1990s and became more integrated with the global economy, more English-speaking employees were needed. The preference for English speakers, especially in the private sector, continued to shift labor migration patterns with a marked decrease in Arab expatriate labor migration and an increase in migration of workers from the Indian subcontinent and Southeast Asia (Yousef 2005). Southeast Asian workers provided a low cost English-speaking alternative for skilled service sector labor especially in the hospitality, security, and medical sectors, as well as unskilled or low skilled domestic servants, drivers, cleaners, and laborers. So expansive was the inclusion of Indian subcontinent and South Asian workers in the GCC economies that the remittances sent back to home countries comprised a significant part of the national economies of the countries receiving remittances (Willoughby 2006). Remittances are discussed in more detail in Chap. 7.

In the mid-2010s, English-speaking African nationals were increasingly incorporated into the labor market to fill service sector jobs. The shift to migrant workers from African countries such as Kenya, Uganda, Nigeria, Uganda, and Comoros occurred because the improved educational opportunities in those countries produced workers who could function in English, the official language in many African countries, and who had basic computer skills (Matthews 2015). The shift from workers from the Indian subcontinent and Southeast Asia was partially caused by their own governments increasing regulations and establishing minimum wages making their nationals less attractive to employers in the UAE. Table 2.4 lists the minimum wages established by governments supplying large numbers of migrant workers to the UAE.

African nationals, many of whom were Muslim, faced with dire conditions in their own counties accepted the wages and increasing filled the void, especially in service sector jobs.

As the expatriate investors, business people, and workers arrived in the UAE to take advantage of the economic opportunities, a population imbalance occurred and previously mentioned in Chap. 1. Figures from the UAE National Bureau of

Table 2.4 Minimum salaries for established by migrant exporting countries (Dubai salary and pay scale 2016)

	Minimum monthly salary	Minimum monthly salary
County providing workers	AED	US$
Bangladesh	750	204
India	1100	300
Indonesia	800	218
Philippines	1400	381
Sri Lanka	850	232

Table 2.5 Population composition from 2006 to 2010 (Government of UAE 2011)

Year	Total population	Expatriate population	Emirati population	Percentage of non-nationals (%)
2006	5,012,384	4,161,220	851,164	83.0
2007	6,219,006	5,341,265	877,741	85.9
2008	8,073,626	7,168,769	904,857	88.8
2009	8,199,996	7,266,615	933,381	88.6
2010	8,264,070	7,316,073	947,997	88.5

Statistics, *Population Estimates 2006–2010* (Government of the UAE 2011) show that although the Emirati population steadily increased from 2006 to 2010, the percentage of Emiratis in the total population steadily decreased during the same period as shown in Table 2.5.

World Bank (2014) figures were slightly higher estimating that by 2012 Emiratis comprised around 18 % (about 1.8 million) while expatriates comprised around 82 % of the country's estimated total population of about 8.2 million people, yet Emiratis still comprised less than 10 % of the workforce. All reports support the United Nations (UN) report that in 2013 "the UAE had the fifth-largest international migrant stock in the world" (Malit and AlYouha 2013). The impact of wage remittances of the large migrant population on the economy of the UAE is discussed in Chap. 7.

2.5 International Attention

Diversification efforts enabled the modern day UAE to become a popular destination for professional development, leisure activities, domestic and foreign investment, and expatriate employment earning international attention in multiple areas including professional development and academia, sports, and entertainment.

2.5.1 Professional Development and Academia

The UAE has become a popular destination for professional development and career enhancement activities. A wide variety of conferences, seminars, workshops, and international summit meetings are held annually in the world class venues on offer in the country. In 2016 more than 50 international conferences covering various disciplines were scheduled with even more planned for 2017 (UAE Conferences 2016).

The UAE attracts domestic and international students wishing to earn post-secondary degrees from the more than 160 private and public colleges and universities operating in the country. In recent years, prestigious colleges and universities from Europe and North America have established branch campuses in the UAE making a high quality Western education more accessible to Emirati and international students of the region (List of colleges 2016; Top Universities 2016).

2.5.2 Sporting Events

Major international sporting events have been held in the UAE in nearly every sport imaginable. For example, soccer fans viewed the FIFA Club World Cup 2010, the FIFA Club World Cup 2009, and the FIFA U-20 World Cup in 2003 broadcasted from the UAE (UAE to host 2015).

Table 2.6 lists a few of the international sporting events held the years 2015–16, along with the websites describing the specific events, demonstrating the variety of different sporting events held in the UAE each year.

Many sports competitions are held during the winter months to avoid the blistering summer heat. However, indoor temperature controlled facilities are available so that competitions can be run any time of year for variety of sports including football, tennis, swimming, ice skating, bowling, billiards, cricket, rugby, martial arts, and basketball. Outdoor endurance sports that attract visitors to the UAE include camel racing, kayaking through the mangroves, car rallies, golf, horse riding, polo, rock climbing, archery, and wide variety of water sports (UAE National Medial Council 2016).

2.5.3 Film Industry

In recent years, the UAE has attracted the attention of film-makers seeking interesting, iconic, and exotic backdrops for their productions. The Dubai Film and TV Commission estimates that more than 6000 feature films, television series episodes, commercials, and corporate videos have been produced in Dubai alone since 2005 (Filming in Dubai 2016). For example, episodes of popular

Table 2.6 Selected international sporting events held in UAE in 2015–16

Event	Source website
Dubai World Cup Horserace "World's richest horserace"	visitdubai.com
HSBC Golf Championship	abudhabigolfchampionship.com
Dubai Sports World 2016	dubaisportsworld.ae
Dubai Tour 2016 Cycling Competition	dubaitour.com
Abu Dhabi Cycle Race 2	abudhabievents.ae
UM Class 1 World Powerboat Championship	class-1.com
Dubai Fitness Championship	dxbfitnesschamps.com
Nad Al Sheba Sports Tournament	nasst.ae
2016 Abu Dhabi Tour	abudhabitour.com
14th World University Chess Championship	wucchess2016.com
DP World Golf Tour Championship	dpwtc.com
Formula 1 Etihad Airways Abu Dhabi Grand Prix	yasmarinacircuit.com
Emirates Airlines Dubai Rugby Sevens	dubairugby7s.com
Mubadala World Tennis Championship	mubadalawtc.com

series *Top Gear*—A British motoring series, *The Bold and the Beautiful*—an American daytime soap opera, and *The Amazing Race*—an American reality TV program were filmed between the years of 2013–2014 (Most Popular 2016).

Areas of the county that have attracted feature film crews include the emirates of Abu Dhabi, Dubai, and Ras Al Khaimah. Productions have featured shots filmed in the emirate of Abu Dhabi including the metropolitan areas of the capital city of Abu Dhabi, salt flats in the desert, and the mountainous areas surrounding the city of Al Ain. In the emirate of Dubai, filming locations have included the commercial district of the city of Dubai and iconic structures such as Burj Khalifa—the world's tallest skyscraper. The unspoiled natural areas of the emirate of Ras Al Khaimah have attracting film crews as well. Table 2.7 lists a few of the well-known Hollywood and Bollywood film productions featuring scenes filmed in the UAE in the last decade.

2.5.4 World Expo 2020

Attesting to the country's economic growth and stability, the UAE won the bid to host the 2020 World Expo, frequently referred to in the UAE as Expo 2020, an international economic gathering to be held in Dubai from October 20, 2020 through April 10, 2021. The expo organizers expect to attract over 200 participants and experience over 25 million visits with around 70 % of all visitors coming from outside the UAE. The area chosen to house the expo consists of a 4.38 km^2 area

Table 2.7 Selected high profile movies filmed in the UAE (Fernandes 2005; Fitzgerald 2016; Most Popular 2016; Filming in Dubai 2016)

Name of film	Location/features
Kung Fu Yoga (2017)	Locations in Dubai
Geostorm (2017)	Dubai
Independence Day: Resurrection (2016)	Featuring Dubai including Burj Khalifa
Airlift (2016)	Abu Dhabi
War Machine (2016)	Several Abu Dhabi locations
Star Trek Beyond (2016)	Areas in Dubai featured as futuristic “vertical” city
Dishoom (2016)	Mountains in Ras Al Khaimah
Ki and Ka (2016)	Featuring Dubai Mall and fountain area in Dubai
Star Wars: The Force Awakens (2015)	Desert in Abu Dhabi
Welcome Back (2015)	Dubai and Al Ain
Furious 7 (2015)	Abu Dhabi
Diamond Necklace (2012)	Dubai
Mission Impossible: Ghost Protocol (2011)	Famous Burj Khalifa scene with Tom Cruise
Wall Street: Money Never Sleeps (2010)	Dubai
Race (2008)	Shots from Al Ain, Jabel Hafeet Mountains
The Kingdom (2007)	Abu Dhabi

located in the Dubai South district located near Al Maktoum International Airport, one of two international airports located in the emirate of Dubai according to the Official Website for the Expo 2020 (Expo 2020 2016).

Construction contracts related to preparing for Expo 2020 include an extension of the Dubai Metro—a driverless automated above ground public transport system, and over 10.6 billion AED (US$ 2.8 billion) in other major project contracts. Projects for Expo 2020 are expected to stimulate the construction industry still recovering from the economic downturn of 2008–2009. In a show of support for the World Expo 2020, private sector developers contributing to the Expo 2020 construction projects have committed themselves to complete their work ahead of the Expo 2020 preparation schedule (Fahy 2016).

Expo 2020 is anticipated to be a catalyst for entrepreneurial activity and apprenticeship opportunities for Emirati young people, so the leadership of the country plan to fully integrate the Emirati youth, especially young Emirati adults seeking employment, into the Expo 2020 preparation and events. Planned activities include roadshows and workshops at post-secondary institutions in the UAE to increase awareness of the ways in which potential job seekers may benefit from Expo 2020 and to build momentum for the event (Pamadero 2016).

2.6 Economic Development Indicators and Regional Corporate Business Hubs

Various economic achievements combined to earn the UAE international attention including achieving milestones in international economic indicators and increasing international economic rankings. For example, the UAE ascended from 27th to 12th in the Global Competitiveness Index ranking in only four years (Schwab 2014). Table 2.8 chronicles the year by year increase in rankings from the year 2011 to the year 2014.

With investment-friendly economic policies and the establishment of Free-Zone areas, the UAE has attracted the attention of multinational corporations seeking to expand into the Middle East and North Africa (MENA) and Gulf Cooperation Council (GCC) regions. Table 2.9 lists a few of the well-known multinational corporations representing a variety of industries that have established headquarters or regional hubs in the UAE.

Table 2.8 Global competitiveness index rankings (Schwab 2014)

Year	Rank (Total)	Score from 1 (Lowest) to 7 (Highest)
2014–2015	12 (out of 144)	5.3
2013–2014	19 (out of 148)	5.1
2012–2013	24 (out of 144)	5.1
2011–2012	27 (out of 142)	4.9

Table 2.9 International companies with headquarters or regional hubs in UAE (Revealed: Top 10 2015; Companies Move Headquarters 2015; Top 10 Firms 2011)

Company name	Sector
Bayt.com	Communications/technology
Continental	Manufacturing
Dulsco LLC	HR and industrial services
Fed Ex	Transportation
Global Hotel Alliance	Hospitality
Halliburton Co.	Energy
LuLu Group International	Foodstuff and retail
Marriott	Hospitality
Merck Serono	Pharmaceuticals
Microsoft Gulf FZ LLC	Communications/technology
Pepsi Co Asia, Middle East and Africa	Food and beverage
Pfizer	Pharmaceuticals
PricewaterhouseCoopers	Audit, assurance, business advisory services
SHUAA Capital	Financial services
Starwood Hotels and Resorts	Hospitality
Swiss-Belhotel International	Hospitality
THE One	Retail

2.7 Stability in a Troubled Region

Located in the MENA region, the UAE resides in an area full of political, economic, and social tensions. Neighbors to the northwest across the Arabian Gulf include the war-torn countries of the Levant (Syria, Lebanon, and Palestine) and Iraq. Just across the Arabian Gulf to the north lies Iran, isolated from most of the world for the last 30 years. Only recently have the global world players taken steps to normalize relations with Iran (Government of the United States of America 2016). Saudi Arabia, sharing many of the cultural attributes of the UAE, yet less of the social openness, borders on the south. Next to Saudi Arabia, located on the southern tip of the Arabian Peninsula, is Yemen, currently experiencing its own political unrest and social conflict (Dobbs 2016). Just across the Red Sea opposite the UAE are Libya, Egypt, Sudan, and Somalia, all of whom have experienced internal conflicts and issues related to unequal distribution of wealth. In contrast, the UAE has pulled through its nationalization and modernization processes as a moderate Islamic country that is economically strong and open to tourists, foreign investors, and guest workers (Rugh 2010).

Political instability and economic issues have prompted nationals from other countries in the region to migrate to the UAE to make a living. Therefore, both *pull* and *push* factors exist to engage migrant workers in the UAE labor market. As previously mentioned, migrant workers were being *pulled* into the UAE labor market lured by jobs and relatively high salaries. The recent turmoil in the region has also created *push* factors in which the job opportunities in local job markets in countries surrounding the UAE have diminished or in which safety and security issues have prompted workers to migrate to find a more stable living environment.

Facing severe difficulties in their home countries, many expatriate workers are willing to work long hours and accept substandard salaries just to have some type of income or to enable them to keep their families in a safe living environment. Unfortunately, according to some experts some companies may locate in the UAE to take advantage of the circumstances of the unfortunate people in the region by driving wages to the lowest possible level, or by increasing the working hours to the longest possible duration, or by expecting workers to forfeit holidays in exchange for overtime payments on a regular basis (Forstenlechner et al. 2012; Toledo 2013).

To assure a fair and equitable labor market, the UAE has established and strictly enforces the labor laws protecting both Emirati and expatriate workers. Labor regulations include *Article 65 of the UAE Labor Law* which states that "the maximum normal working hours for adult employees shall be eight hours per day or 48 hours per week" and *Article 67 of the UAE Labor Law* which states that if workers are requested to work more than normal working hours, i.e., more than 48 hours per week, then the extra hours must be considered as overtime hours with corresponding overtime pay. The law stipulates that overtime pay must be at least 25 % above regular pay (Bobker 2015).

Some employees complain that their employers violate the labor laws and expect their employees to work overtime hours regularly preferring to pay the overtime differential to avoid the costs of hiring more employees. The government discourages this practice, and the Ministry of Human Resources and Emiratization (MoHRE) follows up on reported cases of forced overtime and imposes penalties on companies found guilty of doing so. The *Analytical Report on Economic and Social Dimensions in the United Arab Emirates 2009* states that:

> The UAE authorities have aggressively investigated and prosecuted employers which violate UAE labor laws, have prohibited companies from doing business with recruitment agencies (both in the UAE and abroad) that charge workers fees for travel and/or employment visas and contracts, have substantially increased the number of inspectors responsible for overseeing the treatment of migrant workers by private companies, and have taken various actions to inform workers of their rights upon arrival to the UAE (Government of the United Arab Emirates 2010a, p. 59).

The combination of the excess labor supply, many of whom have extremely low expectations for compensation packages and working conditions, and the behaviors of companies who are willing to exploit such employees, skew labor supply and demand equilibrium. The result is a downward pressure on salaries in the UAE labor market (Forstenlechner et al. 2012; Toledo 2013).

2.8 Summary

Chapter 2 provides key examples of ways in which diversification efforts have provided avenues for the UAE to gain international attention, which in turn, increases employment opportunities in the private sector. Economic indicators were presented supporting the UAE's stable and growing economy and labor laws were briefly mentioned that safeguard the rights of UAE nationals and expatriate workers in the private sector in an effort to assure a fair and equitable work environment. Chapter 3 describes the sub-economies of each of the seven emirates emphasizing the diversification initiatives and private sector expansion in each.

References

Abdulrahman, A. (2013). *Al-imārāt fī thākira ibnaiha: al-hayat al-ijtima'iyah (The emirates in the memory of its sons and daughters)*. Abu Dhabi: Esdarat.

Ahmad, A., AlRostamani, N., & Matthew, F. (2011). *Building a nation, 40 Years of the UAE in pictures*. Dubai: Al Nisr Publishers.

Al-Fahim, M. (1995). *From rags to riches: A story of Abu Dhabi*. London: London Center of Arab Studies.

Al-Qasimi, S. (1988). *The myth of piracy in the Gulf* (2nd ed.). New York, NY: Routledge.

Al-Qasimi, S. (2012). *Sharjah Air Station: Between East and West*. Sharjah: Al Qasimi Publications.

Al-Sadafy, M. (2010, December 1). UAE oil to deplete in 70 years. *Emirates 24/7 Newspaper Online*. Available at http://www.emirates247.com/business/economy-finance/uae-oil-to-deplete-in-70-years-2010-12-01-1.323594

Al-Sayegh, F. (1998). Merchant's role in a changing society: The case of Dubai, 1900–90. *Middle East Studies, 34*(1), 87–102.

Al-Sayegh, F. (2001). Women and economic changes in the Arab Gulf: The case of the United Arab Emirates. *Digest of Middle East Studies (DOMES), 10*(2), 17–29.

Alwasmi, N. (2014, April 22). Reduce the number of expatriate workers in the GCC, says UAE Minister. *The National Newspaper Online.* Available at http://www.thenational.ae/uae/government/reduce-number-of-expatriate-workers-in-gcc-says-uae-minister

Augustine, B. (2014, June 30). UAE least vulnerable among GCC countries to oil price decline. *Gulf News Newspaper Online*. Available at http://gulfnews.com/business/economy/uae-least-vulnerable-among-gcc-countries-to-oil-price-decline-1.1354071

Behery, M. H. (2009). Person/organization job-fitting and affective commitment to the organization: Perspectives from the UAE. *Cross Cultural Management: An International Journal, 16*(2), 179–196.

Bobker, (2015, February 28). Company breaking UAE labour law for making employee work long hours. *The National Newspaper Online.* Available at http://www.thenational.ae/business/personal-finance/company-breaking-uae-labour-law-for-making-employee-work-long-hours

Companies Move Headquarters to Dubai. (2015, July). Dubai, UAE: OneWorld Mid-East Global Business Services.

Davidson, C. M. (2005). *The United Arab Emirates: A study in survival.* London: Lynne Rienner Publishers.

Dobbs. L. (2016, March 8). *Yemen conflict leaves 2.4 million forcibly displaced.* Geneva: United Nations High Commission on Refugees (UNHCR): The UN Refugee Agency. Available at http://www.unhcr.org/56ded9399.html

El-Saadi, H. (2012). Women and the economy: Pre-oil Gulf states. In A. E. Sonbol (Ed.), *Gulf women* (pp. 147–166). Qatar: Bloomsbury Qatar Foundation Publishing.

Emirati Health and Safety Officers 'Must be Employed in Construction Sector'. (2016, July 16). *The National Newspaper Online.* Available at http://www.thenational.ae/uae/government/emirati-health-and-safety-officers-must-be-employed-in-construction-sector

Expo 2020. (2016). *Official website for the world expo 2020 in Dubai.* Available at http://expo2020dubai.ae/content/expo2020.aspx

Fahy, M. (2016, June 30). Expo 2020 projects set to provide timely relief for Dubai's contractors. *The National Newspaper Online.* Available at http://www.thenational.ae/business/property/expo-2020-projects-set-to-provide-timely-relief-for-dubais-contractors

Fernandes, K. (2005, December 28). Hollywood and bollywood films shot in UAE in 2015. *Khaleej Times Newspaper Online.* Available at http://www.khaleejtimes.com/citytimes/in-the-city/hollywood-and-bollywood-films-shot-in-uae-in-2015

Filming in Dubai. (2016). *Dubai film and TV commission.* Available at http://www.filmdubai.gov.ae/filming-in-dubai

Fitzgerald, C. (2016, January). 7 movies filmed right here in the UAE. *Lovin' Dubai.* Available at https://lovindubai.com/feature/7-slick-movies-you-may-or-may-not-have-known-were-filmed-right-here-in-the-uae

Forstenlechner, I., Madi, M. T., Selim, H., & Rutledge, E. I. (2012). Emiratisation: determining the factors that influence the recruitment decisions of employers in the UAE. *The International Journal of Human Resource Management, 23*(2), 406–421.

Government of the Future. (n.d.). *The official portal of the UAE government.* Available at http://government.ae/en/government-of-future;jsessionid=xJ8AqxuHv0zw5bEqhAYEMQ8G.undefined

Government of the United Arab Emirates (UAE). (2010a). *Analytical report on economic and social dimensions in the United Arab Emirates 2009.* United Arab Emirates National Bureau of Statistics. Available at http://uaestatistics.gov.ae

Government of the United Arab Emirates (UAE). (2010b). *United Arab Emirates vision 2021.* Retrieved from http://www.vision2021.ae/downloads/UAE-Vision2021-Brochure-English.pdf

Government of the United Arab Emirates (UAE). (2011). *Population estimates 2006–2010.* Dubai, UAE: United Arab Emirates National Bureau of Statistics. http://uaestatistics.gov.ae

Government of the United Arab Emirates (UAE). (2016). The UAE and global oil supply. *UAE embassy in the United States of America website.* Available at http://www.uae-embassy.org/about-uae/energy/uae-and-global-oil-supply

Government of the United States of America (USA). (2016, January 16). Statement relating to the joint comprehensive plan of action "Implementation Day" of January 16, 2016. Resource Center: United States Department of Treasury. *OpenGov website.* Available at https://www.treasury.gov/resource-center/sanctions/Programs/Pages/iran.aspx

Heard-Bey, F. (2001). The tribal society of the UAE and its traditional economy. In Al Abed, I. & Hellyer, P. (Eds.), *United Arab Emirates: A new perspective* (pp. 98–116). London: Trident Press.

Heard-Bey, F. (2005). The United Arab Emirates: Statehood and nation-building in a traditional society. *The Middle East Journal, 59*(3), 357–375.

Herb, M. (1999). *Absolutism, revolution, and democracy in the Middle Eastern Monarchies.* Albany, NY: State University of New York Press.

Istaitieh, A., Hugo, A., & Husain, N. (2007). *UAE macroeconomic report.* Dubai: Data Management and Business Research Department. Available at www.dcci.ae

Jasim, S. A. (2012). *The necropolis of Jebal al-Buhais: Prehistoric discoveries in the Emirate of Sharjah.* Sharjah: Department of Culture and Information.

Katzman, K. (2010, June 23). *The United Arab Emirates (UAE): Issues for U.S. policy.* Washington, DC: Congressional Research Service.

List of Colleges and Universities in the UAE. (2016, February 2). *Emirates diary.* Available at http://emiratesdiary.com/uae-tips/list-colleges-uae

Kawach, N. (2003, June 12). *UAE has highest population growth in the Arab World. Gulf News Newspaper Online.* Available at http://gulfnews.com/news/uae/general/uae-has-highest-population-growth-in-arab-world-1.358637

Macris, J. R. (2015, July 30). Population and economic activities in the Arab trucial states: A 1901 accounting. *The Journal of the Middle East and Africa, 6*(2), 165–189.

Magee, P. (2014). *The archeology of prehistoric Arabia: Adaptation and social formation from the Neolithic to the Iron Age.* New York: Cambridge University Press.

Malit, F. T. & AlYouha, A. (2013, September 18). Labor migration in the United Arab Emirates: Challenges and responses. *The Online Journal of the Migration Policy Institute.* Available at http://www.migrationpolicy.org/print/4191#.V3-KW3nr0Wc

Mansour, K. M. (2013, March). *Our monuments narrate our history: Twenty years of archeological discoveries in Sharjah (1993–2013).* [supervised by N. Al-Darmaki & S. Jasim (Eds. & Trans.)]. Sharjah: Directorate of Antiquities and Sharjah Archeology Museum.

Matthews, S. (2015). UAE workers and companies build bridges to Africa. *The National Newspaper Online.* Available at http://www.thenational.ae/business/the-life/uae-workers-and-companies-build-bridges-to-africa

Ministry Mandates Companies to Employ Emiratis in Data-Entry Positions. (2016, July 20). *The National Newspaper Online.* Available at http://www.thenational.ae/uae/government/ministry-mandates-companies-to-employ-emiratis-in-data-entry-positions

Most Popular Titles with Country of Origin United Arab Emirates. (2016). Available at http://www.imdb.com/country/ae

Oil-Price.Net. (2016, March 31). *Crude oil and commodity prices.* Available at http://www.oil-price.net.

Pamadero, R. (2016, May 31). Dubai expo 2020: Opportunities for SMEs and young job seekers outlined. *The National Newspaper Online.* Available at http://www.thenational.ae/business/economy/dubai-expo-2020-opportunities-for-smes-and-young-job-seekers-outlined

Potts, D. T. (2001). Before the Emirates: An archeological and historical account of developments in the region c. 5000 BC to 676 AD. In I. Al Abed & P. Hellyer (Eds.), *United Arab Emirates: A new perspective* (pp. 28–69). London: Trident Press.

Revealed: Top 10 Companies in the UAE in 2015. (2015, November 17). *Gulf Business Online.* Available at: http://gulfbusiness.com/revealed-top-10-companies-in-the-uae-in-2015/#.V1xxIHlf0Wc

Rugh, A. (2010). *The political culture of leadership in the United Arab Emirates*. New York, NY: Palgrave-Macmillian.
Schwab, K, (Ed.). (2014). United Arab Emirates. *Global competitiveness report 2014–2015* (pp. 374–375). Geneva: World Economic Forum. Available at www.weforum.org/gcr
Sherif, M., Kacimov, A., Javadi, A., & Ebraheem, A. (2012). Modeling groundwater flow and seawater intrusion in the coastal aquifer of Wadi Ham, UAE. *Water Resourcemanagement, 26*, 751–774.
Shuey, S. (2016, January 16). Ministerial retreat to focus on an economy beyond oil. *Gulf News Newspaper*. Available at http://gulfnews.com/business/economy
Smith, R (Ed. & Trans.). (2008). *A Traveller in thirteenth-century Arabia: Ibn Al-Mujawir's Tarikh Al-Mustabsir* (Translated from Oscar Lofgren's Arabic text). London: Ashgate Publishers & The Hukluyt Society.
Sonbol, A. E. (2012). Introduction: Researching in the Gulf. In A. E. Sonbol (Ed.), *Gulf women* (pp. 1–24). Qatar: Bloomsbury Qatar Foundation Publishing.
Statistica. (2016, March 31). Average annual OPEC crude oil price from 1960 to 2016 (in U.S. dollars per barrel). Available at http://www.statistica.com/statistics/262858/change-in-opec-crude-oil-prices-seince-1960
Toledo, H. (2013). The political economy of emiratization in the UAE. *Journal of Economic Studies, 40*(1), 39–53.
Top 10 Firms to Work for in UAE. (2011, January 2). *Emirates 24/7 Newspaper Online*. Available at http://www.emirates247.com/business/corporate/top-10-firms-to-work-for-in-uae-2011-01-02-1.336876
Top Universities in the United Arab Emirates. (2016). *4 International Colleges and Universities*. Available at http://www.4icu.org/ae/
UAE Conferences. (2016). Available at http://www.conferenceseries.com/uae-meetings/
UAE National Medial Council. (2016). Sports. *UAE Interact Website*. Available at http://www.uaeinteract.com/recreation/sport.asp
UAE to Host FIFA Club World Cup in 2017 and 2018. (2015, March 20). *The National Newspaper Online*. http://www.thenational.ae/sport/football/uae-to-host-fifa-club-world-cup-in-2017-and-2018
United Arab Emirates. (2014). *The World Fact Book Online Database*. https://www.cia.gov/library/publications/the-world-factbook/geos/ae.html
United Arab Emirates Population 1960–2016. (2016). *Trading Economics Online Database*. Available at http://www.tradingeconomics.com/united-arab-emirates/population
Weiner, M. (1982, March). International migration and development: Indians in the Persian Gulf. *Population and Development Review, 8*(1), 1–36.
Willoughby, J. (2006). Ambivalent anxieties of the South Asian-Gulf Arab labor exchange. In J. Fox, N. Mourtada-Sabah, & M. Al-Mutawa (Eds.), *Globalization and the Gulf*. New York, NY: Routledge.
World Bank. (2014, June 25). *Data Bank Online Database*. Retrieved from http://data.worldbank.org/country/united-arab-emirates
Yousef, T. (2005). The changing role of labor migration in Arab economic integration. *Policy seminar on Arab economic integration: challenges and prospects, February, 23–24, 2005*. Washington, D.C: Center for Contemporary Arab Studies.

Chapter 3
Economic Vision of the UAE

Abstract When the rulers of the Trucial States combined resources to form the UAE, a union was conceptualized in which all citizens living in any of the seven emirates benefitted from the wealth generated by the country's natural resources. The leadership invested in each of the emirates by establishing the physical and social infrastructure enabling each emirate to use its own unique resources to build its own local economy and eventually contribute back to the national GDP. This chapter gives an overview of the UAE economic vision then examines the subeconomies of each emirate illustrating the opportunities and challenges for economic grown in each. The emirate of Abu Dhabi, containing the capital city serves as the political center of the country. The emirate of Dubai is known for its commercial development. The emirate of Sharjah is known for cultivating Arab and Islamic culture. The emirate of Ajman is opening its commercial potential and expanding foreign investment potential. The emirates of Ras Al Khaimah, Fujairah, and Umm Al Quwain have begun efforts to expand tourist attractions specializing in eco-tourism showcasing the geographic attributes of each region including mountains, coastlines, and unspoiled nature areas.

Keywords UAE economic vision · Subeconomies of emirates

3.1 The UAE Vision for 2021 and Beyond

The *UAE vision 2021* document outlines economic vision of the UAE using the principles of sustainable development emphasizing that "efforts to succeed and prosper will not come at the expense of Emiratis' strong and healthy emotional balance" (Government of the UAE 2010, p. 2). The document frames the vision of the country around the four central themes that are meant to encompass all Emiratis regardless of the emirate in which they live. The four themes are listed below with the key objectives summarized beneath each one.

G. Daleure, *Emiratization in the UAE Labor Market*,
DOI 10.1007/978-981-10-2765-9_3

Theme 1: United in Ambition and Responsibility
Overall Goal: An ambitious and confident nation grounded in its heritage.
Key Objectives

- Maintaining and strengthening the common Emirati heritage.
- Preserving Emirati culture which includes the Arabic language and Islamic core values.
- Promoting and strengthening the family unit as the building block of Emirati society.
- Connecting strong family units to form strong cohesive communities.

Theme 2: United in Destiny
Overall Goal: A strong union bonded by a common destiny.
Key Objectives

- Ensuring that the resources of the country facilitate sustainable growth and development in all of the seven emirates.
- Assuring an acceptable standard of living among all Emiratis.
- Maintaining personal safety and national security.
- Enhancing international communication and cross-cultural understanding.

Theme 3: United in Knowledge
Overall Goal: A Competitive Economy Driven by Knowledgeable and Innovative Emiratis.
Key Objectives

- Assuring that education and employment opportunities are available to Emiratis desiring to join the workforce.
- Enabling Emiratis to obtain higher levels of education.
- Continuing the progress toward a sustainable and diversified economy.
- Using innovation, research, science, and technology as the basis of continuing progress toward a knowledge-based economy where mutually beneficial partnerships are established between public and private sector entities.

Theme 4: United in Prosperity
Overall Goal: A nurturing and sustainable environment for quality living.
Key Objectives:

1. Continuing the upgrade of healthcare services, educational opportunities, and recreational activities.
2. Preserving natural environments and encouraging conservation efforts.

The *UAE Vision 2021* (Government of UAE 2010) document spells the aspirations of the country's leadership and its commitment to its citizens. It confirms the government's commitment to provide and continually upgrade the country's physical infrastructure and social services systems to maintain a high standard of living in the country. Finally, it reminds citizens of the country's remarkable progress and the effort that must come from all to perpetuate it.

To assure that the country is making progress toward its goals, the UAE government maintains an official website (https://www.vision2021.ae/en/national-priority-areas/national-key-performance-indicators) listing the four themes with government Key Performance Indicators (KPIs) and periodically posts the progress made toward achieving KPIs. For each KPI, the website lists the

1. Index number (KPI in serial order listing)
2. Indicator Term
3. Definition of the indicator
4. Source of information providing evidence of progress toward indicator
5. Most recent results
6. 2021 targets
7. Government authority or department for which the responsibility of the indicator has been assigned.

The website contains a wealth of information not only for Emiratis to chronical the progress of their country, but also for anyone interested in knowing more about the UAE including researchers, potential investors, tourists, and people considering relocating to the country for employment. An example of the information available on the website is presented in Table 3.1 which lists a few examples of the KPIs under the theme of *Competitive Knowledge Economy.*

The selected KPIs emphasize that the growth and development of the UAE is dependent on the growth and development of each of the seven emirates with federal funds supporting emirate-level development efforts. Each of the seven emirates has its own unique features that set it apart from the other emirates. The remaining subsections of this chapter briefly describe the subeconomies of each of the seven emirates highlighting contrasts in the resources of each emirate and the corresponding diversification efforts underway in each one.

3.2 The Emirate of Abu Dhabi

The emirate of Abu Dhabi contains the capital city of Abu Dhabi and the city of Al Ain which is an agricultural oasis irrigated mostly by underground water sources. Abu Dhabi has the most proven oil reserves and contributes about 60 % of the national budget with an annual growth rate in 2013 of about 8 %. The population of Abu Dhabi was about 2.5 million 2015. Diversification efforts in Abu Dhabi include cultural tourism, aviation, manufacturing, media, healthcare, financial services and renewable energy (Istaitieh et al. 2007; UAE News and Information Guide n.d.).

The *Abu Dhabi Policy Agenda 2007/2008* document (Government of Abu Dhabi 2007) identified nine central areas to serve as the overriding goals for the emirate's social, political, and economic planning. According to the document, planning efforts should strive to achieve

Table 3.1 Selected KPIs and results for the vision 2021 theme competitive knowledge economy (Government of UAE 2010)

KPI number 2	Indicator: Gross National Income (GNI) per capita
Definition of indicator	An indicator that measures the real annual economic growth of all sectors except oil. GDP includes the total value of annual production of goods and services
Source of information	World Bank
Most recent results	Rank 3 (2014)
2021 targets	Among the top 10 countries
KPI number 4	Indicator: Global Competitiveness Index
Definition indicator	A composite indicator that measures the competitiveness of countries based on (12) perspectives: institutions, infrastructure, macroeconomic environment, health and primary education, higher education and training, goods market efficiency, labor market efficiency, financial market development, technological readiness, market size, business sophistication, and innovation
Source of information	World Economic Forum—Global Competitiveness Report
Most recent results	Rank 17 (2015–2016 Report)
2021 targets	Among the top 10 countries
KPI Number 5	Indicator: Share of UAE Nationals in the Workforce
Definition indicator	An indicator that measures the share of employed UAE nationals out of the total workforce (expatriates and nationals), across all sectors
Source of information	The National HR Development & Employment Authority (TANMIA)
Most recent results	5.0 % (2014)
2021 targets	8 %

1. premium education, healthcare and infrastructure assets
2. a large empowered private sector
3. a sustainable knowledge-based economy
4. an optimal, transparent regulatory environment
5. a continuation of strong and diverse international relationships
6. the optimization of the emirate's resources
7. premium education, healthcare, and infrastructure assets
8. complete international and domestic security
9. maintaining Abu Dhabi's values, culture, and heritage (p. 13).

The *Abu Dhabi Economic Vision 2030* (Government of Abu Dhabi 2008), "based on the principles laid out in the Government's Policy Agenda published in August 2007, … is a roadmap for the emirate's economic progress" (p. 5) listing seven objectives for continuing economic development including

1. expanding economic development by building an open, efficient, effective, and globally integrated business environment
2. adopting disciplined fiscal policies that are responsive to economic cycles
3. establishing a resilient monetary and financial market environment with manageable levels of inflation
4. driving significant improvement in the efficiency of the labor market
5. developing a sufficient and resilient infrastructure capable of supporting anticipated economic growth
6. developing a highly skilled, highly productive workforce
7. enabling financial markets to become the key financiers of economic growth (p. 45).

Points 4 and 6 specifically address issues related to Emiratization and the UAE labor market and are elaborated upon as "the creation of higher-value employment opportunities, especially for Nationals, and maximizing participation of women in the workforce" (Government of Abu Dhabi 2008, p. 5). In the economic vision, the government of Abu Dhabi stresses the importance of improving the efficiency of the labor market while at the same time developing a highly skilled and highly productive workforce in which Emiratis are expected to fully participate.

The *Abu Dhabi Economic Vision 2030* aims to increase efforts in the tourism and culture sectors (Government of Abu Dhabi 2008). To do so, the Abu Dhabi Tourism and Culture Department was established with its core business areas defined as "creating an infrastructure to support and nurture a sustainable tourism industry in Abu Dhabi, promoting and preserving the emirate's distinctive heritage and culture, attracting visitors and investment and enriching the lives of residents by developing Abu Dhabi as a world-class destination" (Government of Abu Dhabi 2016, p. 1). To achieve these goals, a program consisting of preservation and development has been developed to attract "high-end cultural, sporting and entertainment events, achieved through a network of sponsorships and partnerships with both the private and public sectors" (p. 1).

Evidence of movement toward diversification in the tourism area can be seen in the increase in venues for high-end tourism and event facilitation even though some experts criticized the move. Warning that tourism in GCC in general, and Abu Dhabi specifically, may not be advantageous, Sharpley (2002) advises that

> Despite the apparent advantages that tourism offers over other economic sectors, gaining a share of the global tourism market may be a complex and expensive process, and a significant degree of government support and commitment also may be needed. Thus, in some circumstances, economic diversification may be better achieved through development of alternative economic activities, such as free zones, transport services, financial services, and so on. (p. 234)

Contrary to the warning, evidence indicates that Abu Dhabi is growing as a high-end tourism destination. One indicator of success is the increasing number of hotels that have opened including 35 rated as 4-star and 39 rated as 5-star (Government of Abu Dhabi 2016). Another indicator of success includes the diversity of nationalities staying the hotels. The top 10 nationalities of guests

Table 3.2 Top ten nationalities of guests visiting Abu Dhabi Hotels in January 2016 (Government of Abu Dhabi 2016)

Guest nationality	Number of guests per nationality	Percentage of total guests per nationality	Growth from 2015–2016
UAE	121,780	33 %	10 %
India	24,275	7 %	19 %
China	20,653	6 %	1 %
UK	16,862	5 %	−2 %
KSA	16,308	4 %	12 %
USA	13,308	4 %	6 %
Germany	12,406	3 %	−2 %
Egypt	9498	3 %	23 %
Philippines	8587	3 %	18 %
Jordan	6875	2 %	23 %

staying in Abu Dhabi Hotels along with the guest numbers for the month of January 2016 are shown in Table 3.2.

Table 3.2 shows that Emiratis comprised one-third of the guests that stayed in Abu Dhabi Hotels in 2015, followed by guests from India then China. The highest percentage increases were from the Arab countries of Egypt and Jordan both at 23 %.

The Abu Dhabi emirate's diversification efforts include establishing world-class healthcare facilities and establishing international higher educational institutions by partnering with existing institutions to extend their unique learning experiences into the context of the UAE. One example is the Paris Sorbonne University—Abu Dhabi, wholly owned by the Abu Dhabi Education Council, established in 2006. The institution offers degrees history, art history, music, geography, planning, arts, civilization studies, philosophy, sociology, information and communication in social sciences, humanities, and fine arts at the Licentiate, Masters and Ph.D. qualification levels with all programs delivered in French by tutors from the Paris Sorbonne University (Government of Abu Dhabi 2010).

Another example is New York University Abu Dhabi (NYUAD) whose vision advocates an active connection to its New York site of origin and its other global sites (http://nyuad.nyu.edu/en/). The Sheikh Mohamed bin Zayed Scholars Program (SMSP) is an innovative program run out of NYUAD that offers selected university students from the three participating federal universities, the Higher Colleges of Technology, United Arab Emirates University, and Zayed University, "unique access to specially designed courses, lectures, leadership experiences, networking, graduate school counseling, and advanced degree scholarship opportunities" both in the UAE and during special courses in the USA (http://nyuad.nyu.edu/en/academics/community-programs/smsp/about.html).

3.3 The Emirate of Dubai

The population of the emirate of Dubai in 2012 was about 2.1 million people. Oil accounts for only about 2 % of the emirate's annual budget while Dubai contributes nearly 30 % of the UAE annual national budget. Diversification efforts include trade, transport and logistics, retail, tourism and banking, representing a successful model of diversification and moving the emirate away from dependency on oil. Dubai's successful bid for World Expo 2020 exemplifies the international confidence in the emirate's economic base contributing to the overall economic stability of the UAE (UAE News and Information Guide n.d.).

The *Highlights: Dubai Strategic Mission 2015* (Government of Dubai n.d.) document lists the following five key objectives for continued development:

1. achieving comprehensive development and building human resources
2. promoting economic development and government modernization
3. sustaining growth and prosperity
4. protecting Nationals' interests, public interest and well-being
5. providing an environment conducive for growth and prosperity in all sectors.

Extensive diversification efforts combined with the financial cushion of federal resources enabled Dubai to come through the economic downturn showing an overall GDP growth of 4.5 % in 2012 as mentioned in Chap. 2.

Buckley and Hanieh (2014) comment on the strength of the financial sector, consisting in a large part of Islamic banks and financial institutions, in supporting the stability of the UAE during the financial crisis. Since Islamic financial concepts treat money as an intermediary to facilitate transactions for goods rather than a generator of interest revenue in itself, Islamic banking encourages investments in enterprises with hard assets such as real estate. Buckley and Hanieh continue stating that the Islamic banking institutions facilitate the development of "large, state-backed real estate projects [which] have offered both a permissible and highly lucrative set of investments for Islamic capital" (p. 158). Examples of the large-scale projects planned for the future in Dubai include

> Mohammed Bin Rashid City (MBRC), a joint project of Emaar and Dubai Properties, which is planned to include the world's largest shopping mall (Mall of the World), a Universal Studios franchise, hotel facilities and an enormous public park said to be 30 % larger than London's Hyde Park. As part of MBRC, a gated golf-course residential area is envisioned, with luxury residences on plots of 1,900 to 2,800 m^2 (p. 171)

Construction projects such as MBRC solidify Dubai's commitment to resolving any remaining challenges in the real estate sector showing that "it is adamant in overcoming them and is intent on showing the world that it has not been detracted from its construction boom" (ElHag and ElShazly 2012, p. 404).

3.4 The Emirate of Sharjah

The National Bureau of Statistics reported Sharjah's population in 2009 as 1.01 million people (Government of the UAE 2011). The Emirate of Sharjah maintains a strong manufacturing base and is expanding into developing green businesses and sustainable tourism. The *Economic Vision of Sharjah* indicates an emphasis on cultural and eco-friendly tourism, stating that "Sharjah will be the ideal family destination, aiming to attract more than 10 million tourists by 2021" (Government of Sharjah 2015).

The emirate of Sharjah earned several distinctions in recent years including the *Cultural Capital of the Arab World in 1998*, the *Islamic Culture Capital in 2014*, the *Arab Tourism Capital in 2015*, and the *Capital of Arab Press in 2016.* In addition, Sharjah was ranked in several categories as one of the Top Ten Small and Mid-sized Cities in the *Global Cities of the Future Report for 2014/15* as shown in Table 3.3.

Aided in large part by the efforts of Shurooq, the emirate's investment and development body, Sharjah accounted for around 5 % of the country's GDP and around 8 % of the country's non-oil GDP in 2012 (UAE News and Information Guide n.d.).

3.5 The Emirate of Ras al Khaimah

The emirate of Ras Al Khaimah achieved increased growth rates in recent years with investments in financial services and aviation contributing to an overall growth rate of 8 % in 2012. The National Bureau of Statistics reported the population at about 241,000 in 2009 (Government of the UAE 2011).

Diversification efforts have earned Ras Al Khaimah rankings in several categories as one of the Top Ten small and Mid-sized Cities in the *Global Cities of the Future Report for 2014/15* as shown in Table 3.4.

The rankings in Table 3.4 reflect the accomplishments of the leadership of Ras Al Khaimah including promoting a diversified economic base consisting of

Table 3.3 Top 10 small and mid-sized cities—ranked categories for Sharjah (Global Cities 2014, p. 26)

Rank	Category
6	Connectivity
7	Human capital and lifestyle
8	Cost effectiveness
9	Overall rankings
9	Economic potential
10	Business friendliness

Table 3.4 Top 10 small and mid-sized cities—ranked categories for Ras Al Khaimah (Global Cities 2015, p. 26)

Rank	Category
5	Connectivity
7	Cost effectiveness
8	Overall rankings
9	Human capital and lifestyle
9	Economic potential
9	Business friendliness

corporate enterprises including Julphar Pharmaceuticals and RAK Ceramic resulting in a per capita GDP increase of more than 50 % from 2004 to 2007 (Government of Ras Al Khaimah n.d.).

3.6 The Emirate of Fujairah

The emirate of Fujairah plays a supporting role in the petroleum industry via a recently completed pipeline from Abu Dhabi which opened 2012. The emirate has a liquefied gas terminal and one oil refinery with construction of a second oil refinery in the planning stages.

The strategic location of Fujairah on the Gulf of Oman, just outside the Straits of Houmuz, enabled the emirate to develop as a hub for trading and a storage location for oil and petroleum products. The location attracts large livestock shipping companies and serves as a hub for shipping cows and sheep in the MENA region. All these efforts earned Fujairah the distinction of being the second largest bunkering port in the world (UAE News and Information Guide n.d.).

A significant growth in the tourism and hospitality sector has occurred with hotels and resorts opening in the mountains and at the seacoast. Tourism efforts have been enhanced by the construction of highways through the mountains reducing the travel from Fujairah to Sharjah to about 90 min and from Fujairah to Dubai to less than two hours (Government of Fujairah n.d.).

3.7 The Emirate of Ajman

The population of the emirate of Ajman was reported by the National Bureau of Statistics as 250,000 in 2009 (Government of the UAE 2011). The diversification efforts carried out in the emirate of Ajman include investments in its ports, roads, the transportation sector, and industrial areas.

Reports indicate that one-third of the budget of Ajman for the fiscal year 2016 was allocated to the economic sector to facilitate projects to promote further growth in the emirate (Ajman budget 2015). The *Ajman Strategic Mission 2015–2021* document advocates establishing partnerships to increase tourism and hospitality. As result new higher end hotels were built on Ajman's coast (Government of Ajman n.d.).

To achieve growth by increasing foreign investment in the emirate, the leadership of Ajman allows 100 % freehold ownership of properties for foreign investors. As a result, residential and commercial construction projects have increased in recent years (UAE News and Information Guide n.d.).

Figures from the *2014 Annual Economic Report* released by the Department of Economic Development of Ajman indicate that from 2012 to 2013, the economy of Ajman grew by 5 %, with a GDP increase from AED 15,690 million in 2012 to AED 16,414 million in 2013. Growth in the real estate, hospitality, and business services sectors reportedly contributed 11 % to the budget of the emirate while the transport, storage, and communications sectors contributed about 6 % of emirate's budget (Dubai PR Network 2015).

3.8 The Emirate of Umm al Quwain

The population of the emirate of Umm Al Quwain was reported by the National Bureau of Statistics was 56,000 in 2009 (Government of the UAE 2011). Umm Al Quwain reportedly contributes about 1 % to the national GDP. Industries such as cement, pharmaceuticals, and glass form the basis of the economy of the emirate with plans for the future to include developing an ecotourism industry showcasing the natural environment of the emirate (UAE News and Information Guide n.d.).

3.9 Summary

This chapter shows that the federal government is committed to encouraging growth in all seven of the emirates in the UAE from the emirate with the largest area and the most oil reserves to any of the emirates with much smaller land mass and no oil or gas reserves at all. The economic vision aims to provide the basic infrastructure needed for each emirate to develop in this own way using its own resources. At the same time, the UAE government offers similar services to Emiratis in all of the emirates regardless of the percentage of GDP contributed by the emirate.

Comparison of the subeconomies of each of the seven emirates demonstrates that Emiratis from low population density areas face greater challenges when seeking employment and may be willing to accept lower compensation packages than Emiratis living in higher population density areas with abundant employment opportunities. See Chap. 6 for a more detailed discussion of salaries by geographic location.

References

Ajman Budget for 2016 released. (2015, December 30). *Gulf News Newspaper* online. http://gulfnews.com/business/economy/ajman-budget-for-2016-released-1.1646252

Buckley, M., & Hanieh, A. (2014, January). By urbanization: Tracing the property-finance nexus in Dubai and the Gulf. *International Journal of Urban and Regional Research, 38*(1), 155–175.

Dubai PR Network. (2015, December 9). *Ajman economy grow by 5 % with GDP at 2013 market prices increase to AED 16,414 million*. Available at http://m.dubaiprnetwork.com/pr.asp?pr=105256

ElHag, S., & ElShazly, M. (2012). Oil dependency, export, and economic growth in the Arab Gulf States. *European Journal of Social Sciences, 29*(3), 397–404.

Global Cities of the World Report 2014/15 Winners. (2014, December/2015 January). London: The Financial Time limited. Available at www.fDiIntelligence.com

Government of Abu Dhabi. (2007). *Policy agenda 2007–2008: The Emirate of Abu Dhabi*. Abu Dhabi, UAE: The Executive Council of Abu Dhabi.

Government of Abu Dhabi. (2008, November). *The Abu Dhabi economic vision 2030*. Abu Dhabi: The Government of Abu Dhabi.

Government of Abu Dhabi. (2010). *Economic vision of the Emirate of Abu Dhabi*. Abu Dhabi, UAE: Government of Abu Dhabi.

Government of Abu Dhabi. (2016, January). *Monthly hotel establishment report: Abu Dhabi Emirate*. Abu Dhabi: Abu Dhabi Authority.

Government of Ajman. (n.d.). *Strategic Map 2015–2021*. http://www.ajmantourism.ae/e

Government of Dubai. (n.d.). Highlights: Dubai Strategic Plan (2015). Dubai: Government of Dubai. Available at http://www.sclgme.org/Dubai%20Strategic%20Plan%20-%20English.pdf

Government of Fujairah. (n.d.). Fujairah. http://fujairah.ae/en

Government of Ras Al Khaimah. (n.d.). *Ras Al Khaimah Information Website*. http://rakinfo.ae/government.php

Government of Sharjah. (2015, April 30). Sharjah Commerce & Development Authority Portal. http://corporate.sharjahtourism.ae/en-us/SATC-EN

Government of the UAE. (2010). *Vision 2021*. Abu Dhabi: Government of the UAE. Available at https://www.vision2021.ae/en

Government of the United Arab Emirates (UAE). (2011). *Population Estimates 2006–2010*. Dubai, UAE: United Arab Emirates.

Istaitieh, A., Hugo, A., & Husain, N. (2007). *UAE macroeconomic report*. Dubai: Data Management and Business Research Department. Available at www.dcci.ae

Sharpley, R. (2002). May/June). The challenges of economic through tourism: The case of Abu Dhabi. *International Journal of Tourism Research, 4*(3), 221–235.

UAE News and Information Guide. (n.d.). http://alluae.ae/united-arab-emirates-economy/

Chapter 4
Challenges to Full Emirati Employment

Abstract This chapter explains the development of three distinct sectors in the UAE economy consisting of the private sector, the public sector, and the semi-government sector. During the rapid development phase the public sector and private sectors developed on two tracks with expatriate workers providing labor for the private sector and Emiratis preferring to work in the public sector. The semi-government sector emerged as governmental entities started toward privatization to expand operations and improve services using policies and procedures similar to the profit-seeking private sector companies. Early in the rapid growth phase Emiratis with basic education were easily absorbed into the public sector offering attractive salaries and providing desirable working conditions. However, as the economy began to mature and as the public sector grew saturated, the choicest public sector jobs became scarcer. Chapter 4 presents concerns about Emirati job satisfaction in the public and private sectors, especially with regard to Emirati women and concludes with linking the challenges mentioned in the chapter back to the concept of holistic sustainability.

Keywords UAE economy · Emirati unemployment · UAE labor market

4.1 The First Steps in Post-nationalization Development

After nationalization in 1971, the newly formed leadership of the UAE modernized the traditional concept of the tribal system to include all Emiratis in a tribal community with all members possessing similar rights and responsibilities. The leadership enacted legislation that entitled all Emiratis to benefit from the country's economic prosperity (Herb 1999).

The leadership channeled the newly available oil revenues into projects to accelerate the development of the country and to provide a better life for their people as quickly as possible. The first step was to import foreign models of administrative, financial, and social services structures, communications and transport systems, and trading networks (Al-Ali 2013). As a result, Emiratis

G. Daleure, *Emiratization in the UAE Labor Market*,
DOI 10.1007/978-981-10-2765-9_4

migrated to more densely populated areas to take advantage of the benefits of citizenship which included better employment opportunities and the ability to enjoy the lifestyle upgrades available in the urban centers such as such as sending their children school, having electricity and water provided in their homes, and so on (Alsayegh 1998). The public sector of the urban centers absorbed Emiratis, even those with only a very basic education, however, more labor was needed to maintain the rapid economic growth. Expatriate labor at all levels, from general laborers to highly qualified and experienced professionals, were welcomed as a ready-made solution to fuel the economic expansion and swelling up the non-Emirati portion of the population to more than 80 % of the total population by 2010 (Toledo 2013).

4.2 Formation Multi-sector Economy

The first census indicated that Emiratis comprised about 35 % of the total population at nationalization (about 80,000 Emiratis in a population of about 232,000 people). Only five years later, the total population doubled to about 558,000 reducing the Emirati population proportionately to only about 15 % of the population (UAE Population 1960–2016, n.d.). Due to the large number of non-nationals working in the country, most private sector business transactions were conducted in English necessitating English to become the medium of instruction in federal post-secondary institutions to assure acquisition of the communication skills needed for the workplace (Al-Sayegh 2012).

Up to the early 2000s, Emiratis, even with limited education and experience were readily absorbed into the rapidly expanding public sector and steady oil revenue enabled the government to provide generous compensation packages with desirable working conditions (Sherif 2013). Advantages of working in the public sector included an Arabic-speaking work environment, work based in air conditioned offices out of the extreme heat of the day, relatively short working hours—typically from 7:30 or 8:00 am to 2:00 pm, and jobs of a general service or administrative nature rather than jobs requiring technical expertise or physical exertion (Shallal 2011).

By 2008, the public sector had become saturated and "experienced poor productivity, exacerbated by employment for life for underqualified workers, wasta (nepotism), and a managerial willingness to buy in expertise to tackle problems" (Al-Ali 2013, p. 73). As the workplaces modernized and evolved to accommodate the growing economy, some elements of the labor force were unprepared for the changes or unwilling to make them.

At the same time, concerted diversification efforts earned the UAE international recognition as a destination for upscale tourism, international events, and economic opportunities (Al-Mezaini 2013). Multinational companies chose to take advantage of the political stability and economic opportunities of the GCC region by establishing offices, outlets, branches, or other business entities creating jobs in the private sector. As a result, national income from non-oil revenue rose from 15 % of GDP in 1970 to over 70 % in 2008 (p. 44).

Foreign investment encouraged the growth of a third sector, the semi-government sector, comprised of State Dominated Companies (SDCs), "that have characteristics of private companies but are dominated, organized, and managed by the state" or have the state as a main stockholder (Al-Mezaini 2013, p. 52). Companies in the hybrid sector often offer salaries and benefits similar to the public sector but operate on a profit-generating basis with working conditions similar to private sector companies. The mix of public and private sector characteristics varies by company (Salem and Jarrar 2009).

Despite implementation of Emiratization policies aimed at increasing Emirati participation in the private sector, only minimal results have been achieved (Al-Ali 2013). The private sector business environment evolved with heavy influence from foreign companies which superimposed business practices from their countries of origin. Robertson et al. (2001) explain that foreign business practices are based on foreign values, beliefs, cultural practices, and the economic evolutionary experience of countries outside the region. When indigenous employees are faced with such a scenario, two possible outcomes may result. Indigenous employees may develop *divergence* views which "preserve their culturally unique values despite power of outside influences" or they may develop *convergence* views in which the values of the two distinct groups blend to form a "new set of values, expectations, and behavior based on the dual influences of the trading cultures" (p. 226). As a result, some Emirati employees who preferred to follow the former, felt pressured to adopt the latter perceiving that their cultural values and identity were being ignored or trivialized, thus, making private sector employment unattractive. At the same time, some private sector employers have done little to address the feelings of discomfort, bewilderment, and isolation experienced by Emirati employees, preferring instead to hire from the pool of abundant and affordable expatriate employees available as ready replacements (Pech 2009).

One study by Obeidat et al. (2012) analyzed workplace environments in the Arab region using Hofstede's model for national culture. The findings of the study help to explain the discomfort, bewilderment, and isolation felt by some Emirati employees in private sector workplaces dominated by Western business practices and expectations. The study found that Emirati national culture, as a subset of Arab culture, consists of values, beliefs, perceptions, and practices that are not consistent with those found in the majority of private sector workplaces. Table 4.1 illustrates some of the major areas of interest.

A detailed discussion of the ratings listed in Table 4.1 is presented to fully understand misperceptions that may occur in workplaces in which the corporate structure and culture is different than the employees' culture and expectations. Examples are given where needed.

1. *Power Distance*: A low power distance rating indicates that people expect clear and direct lines to exist between superiors and subordinates with operational policies and procedures clearly defined and strictly followed. A large power

Table 4.1 Comparison of Hofstead's dimensions of culture in mixed culture workplaces (Obeidat et al. 2012)

Dimension	Western context	Arab (Emirati) context
Power distance	Low	High
Uncertainty avoidance	High	Low
Collectivism	Low	High
Masculine/feminine continuum	Closer to masculine	Closer to feminine
Long-term orientation	Advocating long term but acting in short term	Advocating short term but acting in long term

distance rating indicates that people tend to perceive policies and procedures more as guidelines rather than rules to be followed absolutely. The high power distance perception of leadership "emphasizes a dependency relationship between managers and subordinates" (Obeidat et al. 2012, p. 514). It can also mean that those in subordinate positions may not follow the chain of command when seeking resolution to grievances. These differences in perceptions may cause Western supervisors to perceive Arab employees as unmotivated, lacking initiative, and not willing to follow rules. At the same time, Arab employees may perceive their Western supervisors as uncaring, unsupportive, and unwilling to give proper guidance.

2. *Uncertainty Avoidance*: A rating of high uncertainty avoidance signifies that plans will often be intricate and measures are taken to minimize losses in case of failure. Low uncertainty avoidance signifies that planning is more flexible with details often not specified. People with low uncertainly avoidance tend to believe that the future is uncertain, therefore, detailed planning is an unnecessary burden. The differences in perception may cause communication issues or friction between people from the different contexts. Western supervisors may become annoyed when Arab employees reply with "inshallah" meaning "if God wills" rather than an affirmative when asked about meeting a deadline or making an appointment. Arab employees may feel that preparing detailed plans with multiple eventualities wastes time that could be better spend actually making progress toward the goals of the plan. Arab employees may seem less bothered by making exceptions to rules then their Western counterparts.
3. *Collectivism*: A rating of low on collectivism means that competition and ambition in employees is sought and individuals are rewarded with employees being loyal to the organizational goals not their supervisor. A rating of high on collectivism indicates that the "loyalty of employees will be more to their managers than to the organizational goals" and that employees prefer working teams or groups (Obeidat et al. 2012, p. 515). Managers who lack charisma, or are perceived as unsupportive, may demotivate Arab employees. Conversely, Western employees who act on their own rather than in teams or groups may be considered as disruptive to workgroups in the Arab style.
4. *Masculine/Feminine Continuum*: A rating of being close to the feminine side of the masculine–feminine continuum means that people prefer to establish

friendly relationships and consensus in the workplace as exemplified in the phrase "work to life" rather than "live to work" (Obeidat et al. 2012, p. 515). Western employees working in the Arab system may perceive taking time to establish proper relationships as a waste of time leading to misperceptions about productivity. Arab business practices may favor doing business with trusted counterparts even if the individual deals are not the most cost-efficient in the short term. Western business practices tend to favor making short-term deals with cost efficiency the main concern of each individual deal.

5. *Long-term orientation*: People with long-term planning prefer "stable progression toward long-term goals" (Obeidat et al. 2012, p. 516). This concept can be misleading as Western business planning often centers around the long-term corporate health with little regard for the environment, society, or overall sustainability of growth. Although Western businesses may plan for years into the future to secure growth or increase of profits, the effects have often been short-sighted in terms of long-term sustainability often causing long-term damage to the local business context or physical environment which, in turn, may lead to future losses.

The authors summed up that, although Arabs, including Emiratis, "have imported modern laws, rules and structures from others, old (non-Western) practices and customs are still dominant" especially in organizational management styles (Obeidat et al. 2012, p. 519).

Experts including Shallal (2011) and Daleure (2005) found that Emiratis desire a workplace in which their Islamic religion and cultural identity are respected. At minimum, Emiratis expect the flexibility to pray at the appropriate timings with spaces designated for males and females and holidays corresponding to the Islamic calendar. Many Emirati women consider workplaces with shorter working hours or flexible timings as essential because Emirati "women are expected to put their role in the family first" (Al-Ali 2013, p. 49).

One study reported that some Emirati women exited the workforce after experiencing unpleasant aspects of the workplace (Madsen 2010). The women felt uncomfortable and restricted working in close proximity to men because they thought that they would be perceived negatively by other Emiratis in the workplace for talking too much, laughing, or behaving in a relaxed manner in front of men. Additionally, some Emirati women in Madsen's study felt that male colleagues overlooked their contributions and may have felt resentful of them leaving their homes to work.

Sidani and Thornberry (2010) studied work ethic in Arab countries including the UAE and found that the work ethic in many Arabic countries did not seem conducive to economic growth and development. The study found that most challenges stemmed from family dynamics fostering dependence rather than independence, inadequate educational preparation, and leadership structures that promote favoritism rather than rewarding individual achievement.

Toledo (2013) supported Sidani and Thornberry (2010) theorizing that generous social benefits available to Emiratis such as education and health care subsidies, land, and interest-free loans to build houses, and wedding cost assistance contributed to the relatively high unemployment of young educated Emirati young adults. Toledo stated that young Emirati adults entering the workforce do not feel pressure to be financially independent from their families, concluding that financial security and social support "discourage UAE citizens from working" in entry level jobs at a wage acceptable in the labor market yet less than their expectation (p. 40).

Al-Ali (2013) differed in view from Toledo stating that in Emirati culture there is not a specific age that young people become financially independent from parents and families as is the expectation in many Western cultures. According to Al-Ali, a more accurate term for the Emirati context is *lifetime financial interdependence*. Most Emirati families perceive that young people, "have the right to be supported financially by their families" (p. 49). When suitable work is found, young adult males, and increasingly young adult females, are expected contribute to the support of other family members which may include younger siblings, older unmarried females, parents, grandparents, orphans, or other members of their extended families (Daleure et al. 2014; Ridge 2010).

Behery (2009) suggested that to resolve the issue of increasing unemployment of UAE nationals, private sector employers must better align individual characteristics with job duties and organizational goals because all are "related to productivity and commitment" (p. 179). "Many organizations are yet to discover the link between investing in people and work outcomes such as customer satisfaction, high work performance, and profit" (p. 180). Behery concluded that organizations, especially in the private sector, "should continue to look at their socialization tactics to enhance the organizational commitment among their employees" whether Emirati or expatriate employees (p. 191). Salem and Jarrar (2009) advised that "organizational 'carrots' in the form of appraisal systems that incentivize collaboration and sharing of information and knowledge" have allowed the public sector to embrace labor saving technology and enhance work environments and may be used in the private sector in a similar way (p. 8).

4.3 Role of Cultural Sensitivity in Emiratization

Recent studies investigated job satisfaction in the GCC region with mixed results. Although the region attracts so many expatriate workers that citizens are in the minority, low job satisfaction exists in many areas. This section highlights important studies examining job satisfaction in the region and discusses the results for the UAE including results specifically pertaining to Emirati women.

Shallal (2011) investigated the links among demographic factors such as age, education, and income and Emiratis job satisfaction. Similar results were found in both public and private sector employees. Younger employees tended to be less satisfied with their jobs than older employees. Employees with more than a secondary level education tended to be more satisfied with their jobs than employees with secondary or less education.

Overall job satisfaction tended to increase as salary increased in Shallal's (2011) study. However, many Emirati women indicated that they preferred female-only work environments, even if they had to accept lower salaries, so that they could be comfortable and free of cultural pressures exerted by the men in the workplace. Emirati female job satisfaction decreased when working conditions made balancing home and work life difficult. In the study Emirati females emphasized that they were very dissatisfied with work environments that contained pressure from male coworkers to be passive, quiet, restrained, or required tasks that Emirati women perceived to be culturally inappropriate.

4.4 Role of Emiratis in Emiratization

Daleure and Al Shareef (2015) examined Emirati job satisfaction especially among Emirati young adults, by asking Emiratis working in the public, semi-government, and private sectors to rate their satisfaction with 14 job satisfaction criteria. The study found that Emiratis working in the public and semi-government sectors rated job satisfaction criteria moderately high that pertained to salary and compensation, as expected, but they gave very high ratings to job satisfaction criteria pertaining culturally friendly working conditions and flexibility to study and/or take care of family responsibilities. However, findings indicated that a shift in perceptions might be taking place in which younger Emiratis are increasingly considering the opportunities offered in the private sector.

> Respondents who were younger, had spent less time in their current positions, and had shorter careers expressed more satisfaction with their workplace conditions relative to other respondents, while respondents who were older and had spent more time in their current positions and careers expressed relatively more satisfaction with their job security. The greater the number of jobs that a respondent had in his/her lifetime, the more criteria he/she gave high satisfaction ratings; the fewer the number of jobs a respondent had had, the more criteria he/she gave low satisfaction ratings (p. 22).

In other words, older Emiratis appeared to have changed jobs less frequently in their lives than younger Emiratis, yet older Emiratis expressed less overall job satisfaction in multiple job satisfaction criteria. Younger Emiratis appeared to have changed jobs more frequently, but expressed higher levels of satisfaction on multiple job satisfaction criteria in their current jobs. In the study most of the participants who had jobs in the private sector were 35 years old or younger indicating that younger Emiratis may be seeking more fulfillment or financial gain by seeking better opportunities as they accumulate experience.

Elamin (2011) investigated the effects of nationality on the job satisfaction of national and non-national managers in the banking sector. The study found that Emirati bank managers reported higher satisfaction ratings than expatriate bank managers reported. Higher satisfaction ratings were observed in areas of job general satisfaction as well as availability of promotional opportunities, quality of supervision, compatibility of job characteristics, and relationships with coworkers. Elamin explained that Emiratis have successfully integrated and thrived in relatively high numbers in the banking sector. Emiratis display an outward symbol of unity in national dress, share a common values system, and speak the same language with the same dialect. Dissatisfaction experienced by non-Emirati bank managers may have been caused in part by nationalization practices in which non-Nationals perceived that Emiratis were given preferential consideration when hiring and promoting. Expatriate managers may have experienced feelings of isolation, cultural insensitivities, and language barriers causing resentment and low job satisfaction. The study concluded that feelings experienced by the non-national bank managers in organizations with a sizeable number of Emirati employees and managers appeared to be similar to those feelings experienced by Emiratis entering some private sector work environments dominated by expatriate employees and managers.

4.5 Holistic Sustainability as a Framework for Discussing Emiratization

To be successful, economic development must be sustainable. For the economic development to be sustainable, indigenous labor must be fully engaged. The leadership of the UAE realized this concept when they drafted their vision of the model society in the *UAE Vision 2021* document (Government of UAE 2010). The year 2021 was chosen because it is the 50 year anniversary of the nationalization which occurred in 1971. The document emphasizes that economic sustainability cannot be achieved in isolation of cultural, environmental, political, and social sustainability. The concepts in the *UAE Vision 2021* document correspond closely to the holistic sustainability model advocated by Sharma and Ruud (2003). In another definition, Warburton (2003) adds that holistically sustainable practices encompassing the four dimensions of economic, political, social, and environmental must be fully integrated in the corporate environment and must be promoted at all levels of the education system for sustainable development to take place. The remaining chapters of this book discuss the interrelated factors that lead to high unemployment of young educated Emirati adults.

4.6 Summary

This chapter presented the steps toward nationalization that set up the UAE for rapid development. During the rapid development phase the public sector and private sectors developed on two tracks with expatriate workers providing labor for the private sector and Emiratis preferring to work in the public sector. The semi-government sector started to expand operating with government subsidies yet with policies and procedures similar to the profit-seeking private sector companies. The chapter concluded by related concerns about Emirati job satisfaction especially with regard to Emirati women.

References

Al-Ali, J. (2013). *Localizing the GCC workforce: A study and a manual for employers, employees, and job seekers*. Dubai: Masar Printing and Publishing.

Al-Mezaini, K. (2013). Private sector actors in the UAE and their role in the process of economic and political reform. In S. Hertog, G. Luciani, & M. Valeri (Eds.), *Business politics in the Middle East* (pp. 43–66). London: C. Hurst & Co. Publishers.

Al-Sayegh, F. (1998). Merchant's role in a changing society: The case of dubai, 1900-90. *Middle East Studies, 34*(1), 87–102.

Al-Sayegh, F. (2012). Women of the Gulf during the first half of the twentieth century: A comparative study of American missionary archives and local memory. In A. E. Sonbol (Ed.), *Gulf Women* (pp. 241–276). Qatar: Bloomsbury Qatar Foundation Publishing.

Behery, M. H. (2009). Person/organization job-fitting and affective commitment to the organization: Perspectives from the UAE. *Cross Cultural Management: An International Journal, 16*(2), 179–196.

Daleure, G. (2005). Reflections of post-secondary educational experiences of selected women of the United Arab Emirates (UAE): A qualitative investigation of the motivations, supports, rewards, and challenges of seven Emirati women in the year 2004 (Doctoral dissertation, Ball State University). http://eric.ed.gov/?q=daleure

Daleure, G., & Al Shareef, Z. (2015). *Exploring under-representation of young Emirati adults in the UAE private sector by examining Emirati job Satisfaction*. Working Paper No. 9. Ras Al Khaimah: Sheikh Saud Bin Saqr Al Qasimi Foundation for Policy Research.

Daleure, G., Kane, P., Abdalla, H., Rashid, M., Alaskar, S., & Anwar, M. (2014). Using holistic sustainabilityr to preserve cultural identity in the global economic and social environment of the United Arab Emirates. Presented at the 4th Annual Leadership in Learning in the Asian Century conference. Exploring Leadership and Learning Theories in Asia (ELLTA) society, Penang, Malaysia.

Elamin, A. M. (2011). Effects of nationality on job satisfaction: Domestic versus expatriate bank employees in the United Arab Emirates. *International Journal of Management, 28*(1), 20–39. Retrieved from http://www.questia.com/library/journal/1P3-2274272671/effects-of-nationality-on-job-satisfaction-domestic#articleDetails

Government of the United Arab Emirates (UAE). (2010). *United Arab Emirates Vision 2021*. Retrieved from http://www.vision2021.ae/downloads/UAE-Vision2021-Brochure-English.pdf

Herb, M. (1999). *Absolutism, revolution, and democracy in the Middle Eastern Monarchies*. Albany, NY: State University of New York Press.

Madsen, S. R. (2010). Leadership development in the United Arab Emirates: The transformational learning experiences of women. *Journal of Leadership and Organizational Studies, 17*(1), 100–110.

Obeidat, B., Shank, R., Masadeh, R., & al-Jarrah, I. (2012). Toward better understanding for Arabian culture: Implications based on Hofstede's cultural model. *European Journal of Social Sciences, 28*(4), 512–522.

Pech, R. (2009). Emiratization: Aligning education with future needs in the UAE. *Education, Business, and Society: Contemporary Middle Eastern Issues, 2*(1), 57–65.

Ridge, N. (2010, May). *Teacher quality, gender, and nationality in the United Arab Emirates: A crisis for boys*. Working Paper Series 10-06, Dubai: Dubai School of Government.

Robertson, C. J., Al-Khatib, J. A., Al-Habib, M., & Lanoue, D. (2001, August). Beliefs and values in the Middle East and the convergence versus divergence of values. *Journal of World Business, 36*(3), 223–244.

Salem, F., & Jarrar, Y. (2009). *Cross-agency collaboration in the UAE government: The role and impact of technology*. Dubai: Dubai School of Government in partnership with Cisco Systems Inc.

Shallal, M. (2011). Job satisfaction among women in the United Arab Emirates. *Journal of International Women's Studies, 12*(3), 114–134.

Sharma, S. and Rudd, A. (2003). On the path to sustainability: Integrating social dimensions into research practice of environmental management. *Business Strategy and Environment, Social Issue: Corporate Social Responsibility & Governance for Sustainability*, *12*(4), 205–214.

Sherif, S. (2013). Macroeconomic policy, localization, and reducing unemployment: The crucial human resource issues for the UAE. *Competitiveness Review: An International Business Journal, 23*(2), 158–174.

Sidani, Y., & Thornberry, J. (2010). The current Arab world ethic: Antecedents, implications, and potential remedies. *Journal of Business Ethics, 91*(1), 35–49.

Toledo, H. (2013). The political economy of Emiratization in the UAE. *Journal of Economic Studies., 40*(1), 39–53.

United Arab Emirates Population 1960–2016. (n.d.). Online database available at http://www.tradingeconomics.com/united-arab-emirates/population

Warburton, K. (2003). Deep learning and education for sustainability. *International Journal of Sustainability in Higher Education*, *4*(1), 44–56.

Chapter 5
The Roles and Contributions of Women

Abstract The roles and contributions of Emirati women have been acknowledged even before nationalization of the UAE. Women were considered the backbone of society, entrusted with managing families while men were away during pearling season or on trading expeditions. It was no wonder that the leadership of the UAE provided a clear pathway for Emirati women to gain access to education and contribute to society outside the home if they so desired. In recent years, the leadership of the country has gone to even greater lengths to incorporate Emirati women into the workforce by studying reasons for female nonparticipation in the workplace including difficulties maintaining an acceptable home and work life balance. To address the findings of labor market studies, policies to attract more Emirati women into the workforce were developed and implemented. This chapter describes the roles and contributions of Emirati women to the society and economy of the UAE and emphasizes the commitment of the UAE government to educate and provide economic opportunities to Emirati women.

Keywords Emirati women · Role of women in UAE economy

5.1 Emirati Women and the Economic Vision of the Country

In societies around the world, mothers hold a special place as the core of the family and preservers of the culture. Even the term "mother tongue" implies the significance of the maternal influence on society. This chapter discusses the multiple roles of women in Emirati society including the "core of the family" and the "preservers of the culture" and shows how the traditional roles are maturing into the role of "contributors to economic development."

The *UAE Vision 2021* (Government of the UAE 2010) document recognizes the historical and cultural importance of the roles and contributions of Emirati women in society and encourages Emirati women to use the educational and economic opportunities offered in the county to their full advantage. The document also

G. Daleure, *Emiratization in the UAE Labor Market*,
DOI 10.1007/978-981-10-2765-9_5

assures Emirati women that they will not face any type discrimination in the workplace. The document states that

> Respect for Emirati traditions will wholeheartedly support the emerging role of women and continue in helping them to achieve ever-greater empowerment in all spheres. Women will also gain greater opportunity to combine full participation in active life with the joy and fulfillment of motherhood. In pursuit of these noble goals, women will be protected against all forms of discrimination at work and in society (Government of UAE 2010, p. 3).

5.2 Historical Female Roles and Contributions

The economic participation of Emirati women is well documented in political documents and missionary reports of the Trucial States period. In the pre-oil traditional economy, women tended agricultural areas and took care of livestock. In the long absences of men during the pearling seasons, trading trips to other countries in the region, or work abroad, women managed family life and were often solely responsible for the survival of their families and children. Emirati elder participants interviewed for an ethnography study of life before nationalization recalled their memories of women in their lives prior to nationalization (Daleure et al. 2014).

> My father was not there most of the time because of his work, so my mother was doing everything for us to survive, like getting us water, bringing us firewood to warm us and to cook with. She'd wake us up and take us to the sea to wash. She used to feed us dates and she had goats and got milk from them to give us. She'd keep back some of it and put it in a hanging skin and rock it back and forth to make butter from it (EN9).

> My grandmother was doing all the work in the house, breeding the goats, cleaning the house, and cooking the food in pottery (EN16).

> Every woman had to walk to the sea to wash the clothes since there were no machines in those days like washing machines. Women usually helped men by organizing the work in the home, feeding animals, planting some fruits and vegetables, and sewing clothes (EN12).

During the prosperous era of the pearling industry, commoner women contributed to the local economy in ventures outside the home as described in the excerpt from the ethnography study. Not bound by the restrictions of the upper class women, they managed business, owned pearling ships, managed property, even though this brought them into regular contact with men. Some women operated shops and set up retail business with products such as perfumes and incense. Other women learned skills and made money as seamstresses, midwives, traditional healers, or teachers. Women such as Ra'fia bint Hreez, Naiimah bin Humaid of Ras-al-Khaimah became famous for investing their wealth in the pearling fleets and using the profits to establish prosperous retail establishments employing and managing men (Al-Sayegh 2001).

Women sometimes made political contributions from behind the scenes that were strongly felt in society. As an example, Sheikha Salamah, who was the mother of Sheikh Zayed bin Sultan Al-Nahyan, the founding father of the UAE, the ruler of Abu Dhabi from 1966 till nationalization, and the first president of the UAE up to his death in 2004. Shaikha Salamah lived during the time when assassinations were means of ascension, i.e., 1922–1928. One such assassination landed her son Shakhbout in the ruler's seat in the Emirate of Abu Dhabi. Fearing more political instability and wishing to avoid the loss of any of her sons, she made her sons swear an oath not to use assassination as a means of ascension. Honoring her wishes, her sons reconciled and when the time came, power shifted peacefully from Shaikh Shakbout to Shaikh Zayed in the years just prior to nationalization (Heard-Bey 2001).

5.3 Inclusive Education for Women

Even before nationalization, women were included in the social and economic opportunities of the country. In 1956 the first cohort of 30 Emirati women entered formal education, having been sent to Egypt to study with chaperones and by 1958 there were 381 women studying in a similar program. (Government of the UAE, n. d.).

A decade later in 1971 there were around 32,800 Emirati women in formal education. In 1964 the Bureau of Kuwait, then responsible for formal education in the Trucial States, hired two Emirati women to teach in the newly established female schools. Educated Emirati women began entering the workforce in the late 1960s and early 1970s but concerns over the perception that marriage ages would be delayed reducing the number of children born to Emirati mothers caused some women to exit the workforce. Other concerns such as maintaining work and home life balance and the effects of children being raised by servants or someone other than the mother, similar to those experienced by Emirati women today, served to dissuade women from entering the workforce in those early years (Sidani 2005).

After nationalization, education was made compulsory for all Emirati males and females up to grade 10 and free of charge in public schools. Neighborhood schools were established for girls and boys separately with all female administrators and teachers in girls' schools to allay parents' fears of mixing of the genders. Adult centers were opened to provide educational opportunities to women who left the educational system early due to marriage or childbirth, greatly reducing illiteracy among adult Emirati females (Government of the UAE n.d.).

In the early days of nationalization, 350 schools were opened facilitating education of around 94,000 children across the country. When UAE University opened in 1977 approximately 185 students of the first enrolled were female. One effect of these efforts was a substantial decrease in illiteracy in females from 77.6 % in 1980 to 30 % in 1985 (Al-Abed et al. 2008).

When the Higher Colleges of Technology (HCT) and Zayed University (ZU) were established, females were offered postsecondary educational facilities on par with the quality of educational facilities of Emirati males. In fact, many of the

HCT women's colleges are larger than their corresponding male campuses in the same location because the number of women attending outnumber the men and some of the female campuses offer a greater variety of programs to suit the preferences of the women's career choices (Findlow 2007). To further enable Emirati women, busses were organized to provide safe and reliable transportation, if needed, and financial assistance for transportation fees was often provided by local rulers, removing any obstacles to less affluent women (Daleure 2005).

5.4 Women as Largely Untapped Labor Source

Emirati women have entered the workforces in response to encouragement from their leaders. Proactive measures such as extending maternity leaves, reducing the workday by one hour for breastfeeding mothers, and providing on-site day care are ways in which the leadership is making the workplace more attractive to Emirati women (Gallant and Pounder 2008; Nelson 2004).

Some labor market studies including Rutledge et al. (2011) and Toledo (2013) advised that one obvious way to decrease the dependence on foreign labor is to assure that Emirati women, especially young Emirati women with postsecondary degrees, enter the workforce. Kapur (2013) mentions that Emirati women have entered the private sector in greater number than Emirati men, perhaps to avoid the stiff competition with Emirati men for jobs in the saturated public sector.

Despite these measures described in this chapter, many Emirati women, do not wish to enter the workforce. The social value placed on child reading and providing a stable family life provides a value that salary earned working outside the home cannot replace for many Emirati families. In addition, some Emirati women do not feel comfortable in mixed gender work environments and opt out of the workforce (Madsen 2010; Shallal 2011). Emirati women or their families perceive some occupations or industries as unsuitable and although well-paying opportunities exist, therefore, Emirati women avoid may them (Sharpley 2002).

5.5 Emirati Women in the Workforce

Emirati women have been encouraged from the highest level of government and society to obtain as much education as desired and work outside the home. The leadership realizes that one way to decrease the dependence on foreign labor is to encourage Emirati women to work. However, many Emirati women are dissatisfied with their opportunities and opt out of the workforce (Al Suwaidi 2010).

As mentioned earlier, Emirati males are financially responsible for the maintenance of their families and Emirati women are socially and culturally expected to see to the nonfinancial needs of their families. When Emirati women opt to enter the workforce it is often out of financial necessity—to supplement the salary of their husbands, provide extras such as private school for their children, or help support elderly parents (Harry 2007).

However, Emirati husbands do not necessarily reciprocate roles and may not contribute to the care and maintenance of the family in nonfinancial ways. A study investigating the motivations, supports, rewards and challenges for Emirati women entering into postsecondary in preparation for work found that

> Emirati women participated in post-secondary education as a means to achieve self-satisfaction, to assist in developing their country, to provide for themselves and their children if necessary; and to achieve their future goals. Some participants mentioned that post-secondary education gave Emirati women, who had very limited freedom, a chance to become independent (Daleure 2005, p. 172).

Women in the study were acutely aware of their dual roles and had definite preferences for workplace situations corresponding to the cultural expectations of Emirati women. Participants felt that they wanted to work in environments which allowed them to preserve their Islamic identity and were not physically strenuous. As Emirati women consider employment options, they face challenges in achieving an appropriate work and home life balance causing some women to exit the workforce or delay entry until the family situation becomes more supportive.

A recent study, *Brief of Survey of the Needs of Working Women in the Federal Government Sector*, conducted by the United Arab Emirates Authority for Government and Human Resources (UAE FAGHR) investigated job satisfaction criteria for Emirati women working in federal government jobs. The study found that the main sources of dissatisfaction for Emirati women were short maternity leaves, workplaces with inflexible timings, and work times in the evenings or on weekends (UAE FAGHR 2011). Emirati women make up slightly less than half 49 % of the working age population yet only about 15 % of the Emirati workforce. Therefore, Emiratization programs seeking to include more Emirati women have begun addressing reasons for Emirati female nonparticipation to achieve reasonable gender parity in Emirati employment (Sherif 2013).

To understand the situation that Emirati couples face, consider the following case study, variations of which have been reported in the studies mentioned in this chapter and which have been blamed, at least partially, for the rising divorce rates among Emirati couples (Daleure 2005; Elamin 2011; Shallal 2011; Nelsen 2004; UAE FAGHR 2011).

5.6 Case Study of Young Adult Emirati Women and Marriage

Part 1: Background of Case Study

> A recently married fresh business graduate, Noora, applied for her first job in a career fair. She had one of the highest Grade Point Averages (GPAs) in her graduating class but she had no paid work experience. Due to lack of experience, she was overlooked for positions

she applied for in the preferred, yet saturated public sector, and was only offered work in a private sector company. As usual for private sector employment, the company's working hours were from 8am to 5 pm and she was expected to work at least one Saturday each month and take a day off during the week.

Her husband, Marwan, agreed to all the terms and encouraged her to work. Marwan was well aware that if Noora worked and contributed less than half her salary to the household budget, the couple could pay off all the debts they incurred for their lavish wedding party and honeymoon trip the previous year. Noora was very happy to have her husband's support and accepted the offer.

Marwan was a sponsored student in college. When he graduated, he started working immediately in a semi-government company from 7:30 am to 2:30 pm. Not wanting to burden Noora, he started having lunch with his friends and then napped until Noora returned home from work at 5:00 pm or even 5:30 pm if there were meetings. Noora then prepared the evening meal and they spent the evening together.

Variation 1:

The first month or so all went well. Noora enjoyed her new job and Marwan was able to start paying off their wedding loans. Then Noora started feeling unwell and was too tired to prepare dinner when she returned home from work. Marwan wanted to support Noora so he began ordering food or taking Noora out to eat.

A visit to the doctor confirmed that Noorah was pregnant and she missed a few days of work. Her work started piling up and she started to feel stressed. Meanwhile, Marwan started complaining about all the money they were spending by eating out – his lunches with his friends and their evening meals together. When Marwan's family learned of the pregnancy, Marwan's mother insisted that they come for dinner at Marwan's parents' home to take pressure from Noora which seemed like a great solution to Marwan.

After the first few days, Marwan began to droping Noora off at his family's house while he went to the club or gym in the evenings with his friends. Noora felt lonely and frustrated. Noora discussed her frustration with Marwan who became angry telling her that SHE wanted to work, so why was she complaining. She decided to submit her resignation at work. Then she could manage her home, cook the meals, prepare for her new baby, and be available for Marwan so that he did not have an excuse to go out so much with his friends.

Variation 2:

The first month or so all went well. After Noora received her new credit card, she started using it to purchase new shoes and bags her herself and items for their house. At the end of the second month, Marwan saw the credit card bills and was shocked. He discussed the finances with Noora and asked her not to spend so much money because he was counting on her contribution toward their wedding debts.

Noora became angry and told Marwan that he worked less hours than she worked, he made more money than she made, and he received family allowances in his pay package. She asked him why SHE should have to give him any money for the household budget. She then reminded Marwan that family expenses were the man's responsibility so why should he tell her what to do with her salary.

Marwan reminded Noora that he only agreed for her to work because she agreed to contribute to the wedding debts. He advised her to quit her job and stay home if all she wanted to do spend her money and not reduce their debts. Noora felt that Marwan is being unfair and Marwan felt that Noora was being unreasonable. Their relationship became strained and for the first time they considered divorce.

Although the case studies presented are fictitious, the issues presented are real. Young Emirati couples face variations of the scenarios mentioned in the scenarios and a plethora of others as Emirati women consider working outside the home. Emirati women who are offered positions in the private sector jobs often have husbands (or future husbands) who work in the public sector. The wife would, therefore, be working longer hours than her husband and may have a lower salary and less desirable benefits. However, the wife would most likely be responsible for managing the household while her husband will most likely continue with his existing lifestyle and his expectations of his wife's role as primary homemaker (Sidani 2005).

The Emirati legal and cultural expectations hold the males solely responsible for financial maintenance of their families (Simidi and Kamali 2004). This social norm leads some Emirati women to feel that contributing to their family budget is not their responsibility. Some Emiratis, both male and female, believe that the wife's role in the home is more valuable than any monetary compensation could provide, so by working outside the home, women devaluate their time and tire themselves for no good reason, especially if their husbands earn enough to cover their needs. In some cases, the in-laws of young couples, eager to have grandchildren as soon as possible and see the marriages off on a solid footing, may encourage young brides opt out of employment outside the home.

5.7 Summary

The UAE government recognizes the economic benefits of engaging more Emirati women in the workforce to reduce dependence of foreign labor. Although Emirati women have the support and encouragement of the UAE government to earn postsecondary degrees and work outside the home, some Emirati women find maintaining a suitable work and home life balance so challenging that they opt out of the workforce. New labor laws may provide additional opportunities for Emirati women to enter the workforce and maintain a work home life balance.

References

Al-Abed, I., Vine, P., Hellyer, P., & Vine, P. (Eds.). (2008). *United Arab Emirates Yearbook: 2008*. London: Trident Press.

Al-Sayegh, F. (2001). Women and economic changes in the Arab Gulf: The case of the United Arab Emirates. *Digest of Middle East Studies (DOMES), 10*(2), 17–29.

Al Suwaidi, J. S. (2010). Introduction: Education and the Requirements of the GCC Labor Market. *Education and the Requirements of the GCC Labor Market* (pp. 3–8). Abu Dhabi: The Emirates Center for Strategic Studies and Research.

Daleure, G. (2005). Reflections of post-secondary education experiences of selected Emirati women: *A qualitative analysis investigating the motivations, supports, rewards, and challenges of seven Emirati women in the United Arab Emirates* (Doctoral Dissertation). Muncie, IN: Ball State University. Retrieved from http://eric.ed.gov/daleure

Daleure, G., Kane, P., Abdalla, H., Rashid, M., Alaskar, S., Ibrahim, M., et al. (2014). Using "holistic sustainability" to preserve unique cultural identity while participating in the contemporary global economic and social environment: the case of the United Arab Emirates. In *Proceedings of the 4th Annual Leadership in Learning in the Asian Century conference*. Penang, Malaysia: ELLTA society.

Elamin, A. M. (2011). Effects of nationality on job satisfaction: Domestic versus expatriate bank employees in the United Arab Emirates. *International Journal of Management, 28*(1), 20–31.

Findlow, S. (2007). Women, higher education and social transformation in the Arab Gulf. In Brook, C., Levers, L. (Eds.), *Aspects of education in the Middle East and Africa*. Symposium Books.

Gallant, M., & Pounder, J. (2008). The employment of female nationals in the United Arab Emirates (UAE): An analysis of opportunities and barriers. *Education, Business and Society: Contemporary Middle Eastern Issues, 1*(1), 26–33.

Government of the United Arab Emirates (n.d.). *Women in the United Arab Emirates: A portrait of success*. Abu Dhabi: Government of the United Arab Emirates.

Government of the United Arab Emirates (UAE). (2010). *United Arab Emirates Vision 2021*. Retrieved from http://www.vision2021.ae/downloads/UAE-Vision2021-Brochure-English.pdf

Harry, W. (2007, January). Employment creation and localization: the crucial human resource issues for the GCC. *International Journal of Human Resource Management, 18*(1), 132–146.

Heard-Bey, F. (2001). The tribal society of the UAE and its traditional economy. In Al Abed, I., Hellyer, P. (Eds.), *United Arab Emirates: A New Perspective* (pp. 98–116). London: Trident Press.

Kapur, S. (2013, October 23). Private sector jobs alert: Emiratis now more open to joining. *Emirates 24/7 Newspaper Online*. Available at: http://www.emirates247.com/news/emirates/private-sector-jobs-alert-Emiratis-now-more-open-to-joining

Madsen, S. R. (2010). Leadership development in the United Arab Emirates: The transformational learning experiences of women. *Journal of Leadership and Organizational Studies, 17*(1), 100–110.

Nelson, C. (2004). *UAE national women in the private sector: Conditions and constraints. Labour Market Study No. 20*. Dubai: Center for Labor Market Research & Information (CLMRI) & The National Human Resource Development and Employment Authority (Tanmia).

Rutledge, E. J., Al Shamsi, F., Bassioni, Y., & Al Sheikh, H. (2011). Women, labour market nationalisation policies and human resource development in the Arab Gulf States. *Human Resource Development International, 14*(2), 183–193.

Shallal, M. (2011). Job satisfaction among women in the United Arab Emirates. *Journal of International Women's Studies, 12*(3), 114–134.

Sherif, S. (2013). Macroeconomic policy, localization, and reducing unemploymnet: The crucial human resource issue for the UAE. *Competitiveness Review: An International Business Journal, 23*(2), 158–174.

Sharpley, R. (2002, May/June). The challenges of economic diversificationr through tourism: The case of Abu Dhabi. *International Journal of Tourism Research, 4*(3), 221–235.

Sidani, Y. (2005). Women, work, and Islam in Arab societies. *Women in Management Review, 20* (7), 498–512. doi:10.1108/09649420510624738.

Simidi, F. A., & Kamali, M. A. (2004). Assessing the values structure among UAEU students. *Social Behavior and Personality, 32*(1), 19–29.

Toledo, H. (2013). The political economy of Emiratization in the UAE. *Journal of Economic Studies, 40*(1), 39–53.

UAE Federal Authority for Government Human Resources (UAE FAGHR). (2011). *Brief of survey of the needs of working women in the federal government sector*. Retrieved on 12 June 2012 from www.fahr.gov.ae

Chapter 6
Wages, Salaries, and Expatriate Labor

Abstract This chapter takes a look at the composition of the UAE labor market highlighting the proportion of jobs available in various sectors and at various salary levels. Much of the literature available on Emiratization and the UAE labor market reports obtaining a desired salary as a prime motivating factor in Emirati career decision-making. Yet, few studies have investigated the actual proportion of jobs that are available within the desired salary range and whether Emiratis are being adequately prepared to fill those positions. This chapter presents and discusses salary distributions by controlling for different factors using available data sets. The salary data directly and indirectly show that industries and occupations in the private sector, for which Emiratis are being educated and trained, may not be aligned with salary expectations of Emirati job seekers. Evidence presented suggests that a deceptively low number of jobs are actually suitable for Emiratis in terms of salaries and working conditions or in terms of preparation needed to obtain and maintain employment. The resulting intense competition for suitable jobs among jobseekers, Emirati and non-Emirati, supports the need to introduce Emiratization efforts to assure opportunities for young Emirati adult job seekers.

Keywords Expatriate labor in UAE · UAE labor market · UAE workforce · Migrant workers

6.1 Sources of Labor Market Data

Putting together reliable labor market figures such as salaries and working hours per demographic categories such as nationality, education, gender, sector, and so on in the private sector is challenging because collecting this type of information has only recently been attempted. Recent efforts of the UAE government to provide transparency and ease of finding information for research and policy purposes have resulted in repositories being created to house available statistical data.

G. Daleure, *Emiratization in the UAE Labor Market*,
DOI 10.1007/978-981-10-2765-9_6

The last national census for which data was made public occurred in 2005. Since then, individual emirates were tasked with providing census figures for their own constituencies but not all of them had produced the requested data at the time of preparing this publication. Therefore, data gleaned from periodic academic studies provided the best available data to examine salaries categorized by demographic criteria. The most extensive studies were carried out in 2008 and 2009 through the Ministry of Human Resources and Emiratization (MHRE), formerly the Ministry of Labor (MOL) which includes TANMIA, the national employment agency. Reports from private recruiting companies including Bayt.com, Hays UAE, and GulfTalent were used for comparison purposes to supplement the Ministry data. The reports from private organizations were constructed from voluntarily submitted data using convenience sampling so the results may not be generalizable to the overall UAE labor market, however, in absence of systematically collected data from official sources, the reports represented one perspective of the best data available. The results of new studies relating the UAE are gradually becoming available, so the reader is provided with the links to available repositories to continue the search for more up-to-date information if desired.

Although not an exhaustive list, Table 6.1 identifies helpful repositories of data, statistics, and academic papers pertaining to Emiratization and the UAE labor market and the links to find the resources.

The datasets used in this section were obtained from a variety of government statistics repositories and publications published by public and private organizations mentioned in Table 6.1 along with academic journal articles. Because the studies were carried out by varying organizations and for varying purposes, the data is sometimes contradictory and challenging to interpret. In addition, salary estimators or calculators can be found that give salary estimates for specific jobs, educational qualifications, sectors, and so on. Since source studies are not given for the salary calculators, the accuracy cannot be verified, however, as official source reports are not always available, they served as a one source of information to be considered. Some popular examples are listed.

- *Salary Calculator for the Middle East*, provided by GulfTalent at https://www.gulftalent.com/salaries.
- *PayScale*, provided by Human Capital at http://www.payscale.com.
- *Salary Calculator*, provided by Robert Half Recruiting Consultants, at https://www.roberthalf.ae/salary-calculator.
- *Salaries in the UAE*, provided by Bayt.com at http://www.bayt.com/en/salaries/countries/uae/.

One important source of data is the official data set reported by the MHRE for 2008 is the *Employment, Wages, and Hours Worked Survey 2008* (Gov of UAE 2009) consisting of salary and demographic data on more than 1.7 million employees working in more than 16,000 establishments in the UAE and referred to in this section as the "Ministry Study". The year 2008 is last year that complete data figures are available from official sources. Another source used in this section is a

Table 6.1 Data, statistics, and academic publications

Title of resource	Description of resource	Location of resource
Abu Dhabi Statistics Center (SCAD)	Data about emirate of Abu Dhabi	www.scad.ae
Dubai Statistics Center (DSC)	Data about emirate of Dubai	www.dsc.gov.ae
Emirates Center for Strategic Studies and Research (ECSSR)	Academic papers and conference proceedings on topics relevant to the UAE	www.ecssr.ac.ae
Federal Competitiveness and Statistics Authority (FCSA)	Data about UAE but most statistics about wages available only up to 2009	www.fcsa.gov.ae
Fujairah Statistics Center	Data about emirate of Fujairah	www.fscfuj.gov.ae
Mohamed bin Rashed School of Government (MBRSG)	Repository for working papers, policy briefs, and other documents (previously the Dubai School of Government DSG)	www.mbrsg.ae
Innovation Development and Management Consultants (IDMC)	Website tab "Knowledge Center" provides access to studies and research materials including a link to the National Bureau of Statistics (NBS)	www.idmc.ae
Sharjah Statistics Portal	Data about the emirate of Sharjah	www.sharjah.gov.ae
Sheikh Saud bin Saqr Al Qasimi Foundation for Policy Research	Repository of working papers, policy briefs, and other academic papers relevant to the emirate of Ras Al Khaimah and the UAE	www.alqasimifoundation.com
UAE Interact	Supported by the UAE National Media Council, the website provides news about UAE and links to websites and publications	www.uaeinteract.com
UAE Yearbook	Searchable resource with yearbooks up to 2013 with updates posted periodically	www.uaeyearbook.com

report prepared by the Institute for Social and Economic Research (ISER) using data from a survey conducted by the Dubai Economic Council (DEC) in 2008 with 22,416 randomly selected Emirati participants referred to in this section as the "DEC Study" (Tong 2010).

Results of workplace studies conducted and by prepared by private organizations were used to supplement the official reports especially after 2008 since official data is not readily available. Private organization reports include the *Employment and Salary Trends in the Gulf 2016* study in which 25,000 professionals and over 700 executives, human resource managers, and senior executives in the GCC participated (GulfTalent 2016); *Salary and Employment Report: Salaries and Trends of the Growing GCC Market* (Hays 2016) with information from more than 2400 employees and 200 hiring managers; and *2015 Salary Guide* (Morgan McKinley 2016) for selected sectors and occupations.

6.2 General Salary Information

According to the DEC study, the annual median salary in 2008 was 39,000 AED (US $10,626) or AED 3250 (US$886) per month while the mean annual salary was reported at 90,484 (US$24,655) or AED 7540 (US$2055) per month (Tong 2010, p. 6). In the same study, employees reported working an average of 8 hours of overtime weekly which is included in the salary figures. Another source ("Salary survey" 2016) estimates the average monthly salary in the UAE in 2016 as AED 18,175 (US$4952) or AED 218,100 (US$59,427) annually illustrating the wide discrepancy in information available pertaining compensation in the UAE labor market.

Most published reports indicated that salaries have risen steadily from 2008 to 2016 similar to the figures presented in Table 6.2, with the rates of increase slowing each year.

However, some experts expressed concern that falling oil prices had significantly affected wage increases from 2014 to 2016 with actual increases reduced from predicted and they commented that the rising cost of living would serve to negate any increase in purchasing power. As expressed by one report

> Until the very end of 2014 we were looking forward to a bumper year in terms of both the creation of new headcount and salary growth, but we have had to reassess and lower expectations. … Overall we are therefore likely to see a 10-12% increase in the overall number of new jobs, with salaries increasing in line with inflation at around 5-6%. For many, the actual cost of living is outstripping salary increases (Morgan McKinley 2016, p. 3).

Analysists from GulfTalent concurred stating that

> Many professionals in 2016 are likely to face a double-whammy of rising living costs as a result of cuts in government subsidies, coupled with stagnant wage growth due to the depressed hiring market. As a result, real salary increases net of inflation are expected to be significantly lower than in previous years (GulfTalent 2016, p. 11).

Although a useful starting point, figures representing median salaries or mean salaries are not particularly helpful when investigating Emiratization or the UAE labor market because the salaries vary significantly by sectors and employee

Table 6.2 Average percentages increases in base salary in UAE from 2014 to 2016 (GulfTalent 2016, p. 12)

Year	Increase in base salary (%)
2014	6.2
2015	5.6
2016	5.3

demographic factors causing mean and median salary figures to mask the more common extremes at both the low and high end.

According to a report published by the Gulf Labour and Migration Center, top employing sectors for Emiratis from 2008 to 2015 were the Public Administration, Defense and Social Security, and Education sectors collectively employing approximately 70 % of all Emiratis. The top employing sectors for expatriates were the Construction, Service, and Industrial sectors (De Bell Airs 2015). However, as the next subsections illustrate the salary levels vary not only from sector to sector, salaries vary by nationality, occupation, industry, education level, age grouping, economic sector, and gender. Further, salary level distinctions vary within the subgroupings illustrating that the number of jobs desired by UAE nationals is much less than might be expected when viewing the total number of jobs in the economy. In addition, salaries offered are often less than indicated when looking only at mean or median salaries by any one individual factor.

6.3 Salaries by Nationality

Published reports breaking down salaries by nationality can be confusing when multiple nationalities are lumped together in unhelpful categories. Researchers sometimes report findings by grouping nationalities in studies pertaining to the UAE labor market using group schemata similar to international organizations or in ways similar to other studies they have previously carried out. However, as shown in Table 6.3, the nationality groupings do not provide sufficient clarity to accurately conclude relationships between nationality and salary levels in the context of the UAE.

The way that the results of this study are grouped is problematic as published because the groupings used do not allow comparing mean salaries by specific nationality. For example, the category “Oceanic countries” definitely includes Australia, and New Zealand whose nationals tend earn relatively high salaries, but may also include Indonesia and the Philippines, whose nationals tend to earn relatively low salaries. In another example, South American representation in the UAE labor market is very low but those South Americans in the labor market seem to have relatively high salaries most likely because they were hired for some particular expertise at a relatively high salary. A third issue is the grouping of “non-Arab Asian countries” which seem to include nationals from the Indian subcontinent and may also include Turkish nationals, Asian countries that were formerly associated with or included in the Soviet Union, and Persia. Since the groupings were not defined in the study, non-Arab Asian countries may include countries such as Indonesia and the Philippines.

In the DEC study salaries reported by nationality were grouped by region of origin in a different, yet similarly obscure way as follows:

- *Western* (UK, EU, North American, etc.) with annual salary US$85,014
- *Emirati* with annual salary US$58,856

Table 6.3 Monthly wages by nationality for 2008 from ministry study (table constructed by calculating raw data presented in Government of UAE 2009)

Rank	Nationality group	Earnings			Hours worked	
		Monthly (AED)	Annually (AED)	Annually US$	Monthly	Weekly
1	Oceanic Countries	20,689	248,267	67,648	185	42.8
2	North American Countries	20,471	245,654	66,936	188	43.3
3	South American Countries	15,546	186,552	50,832	192	44.4
4	United Arab Emirates	15,064	180,773	49,257	173	39.8
5	European Countries	14,516	174,197	47,465	193	44.6
6	GCC Countries	10,283	123,394	33,622	193	44.5
7	Central American and Caribbean Countries	7997	95,965	26,149	221	51.0
8	Other Arab Countries	7209	86,506	23,571	199	45.9
9	Non-Arab African Countries	6077	72,918	19,869	201	46.4
10	Not Stated	5533	66,398	18,092	200	46.1
11	Non-Arab Asian countries	3215	38,575	10,511	215	49.7

- *Other GCC Nationals* with annual salary US$21,253
- *Non-GCC MENA* with annual salary US$19,619
- *Indian Subcontinent* with annual salary US$6866
- *Rest of Asia* with annual salary US$5886
- *Rest of Africa* with annual salary US$5559
- *Asian Tigers* with annual salary US$2917.

Working hours for the groups ranged from an average of 40 hours per week for the *Western* grouping to 70 hours per week for the *Asian Tigers* grouping. In addition, about one-fifth (21 %) of the participants in the DEC study were Emirati and about half (49 %) were from the Indian subcontinent. However, the workers from the Indian Subcontinent category were mostly low-skilled workers including clerks, office workers, laborers, and domestic servants earning less than one-fifth of the average salary for Emirati workers. Emiratis, on the other hand, were educated at least high school graduates and many were college educated earning five times from 2.5 to 20 times the salaries of all other groups excluding *Western* (Tong 2010).

Results of the two studies support Aydemir (2015) who theorized that expatriate workers corresponding to *Western* category or combined categories of *Oceanic*,

North American, and *European Countries* in the DEC Study and Ministry studies, respectively, earned the highest average salary presumably because they were hired for some specific expertise and require a high salary to be drawn from the labor market in their home countries. The next highest average salary was for the *Emirati* grouping, which was only about half the median salary for *Westerners* yet almost three times the next two groupings, *Indian Subcontinent* and *Asian Tigers*. The *Indian Subcontinent* mean salary was only about 10 % of the *Emirati* salary grouping. The *Asian Tigers* grouping, including Indonesian workers who presumably fall into the category *Rest of Asia* most likely includes nationals from the Philippines, earn the lowest salaries.

Both the Ministry Study and the DEC Study results support Constant (2015) who advised that Emiratis are mostly competing with the expatriates that would fall into *Western* category or combined categories of *Oceanic*, *North American*, and *European Countries* in the DEC Study and Ministry studies, respectively. Even with the grouping limitations, the results of the studies presented support each other in confirming the general trends in previously mentioned literature. Nationalities from English speaking countries earned the highest salaries. Emiratis received the next highest salaries, less than most English speaking nationalities, but more than other Arab nationality groups and more than African and Asian national groups.

6.4 Salaries by Industry and Occupation

Salaries by industrial groupings are presented for 2008 in Table 6.4.

As shown in Table 6.4, public sector industries appear to have the highest average salaries while the professional private sector industries appear to offer moderate salaries. The lowest salaries are offered in the service industry and other labor intensive industries that do not require high skills and educational levels. Other studies including Tong (2010) show roughly the same trends in salaries although the DEC survey dataset reveals a greater disparity between the highest salaries and the lowest salaries. As can be quickly realized, the top salaries by industry are much lower than the top salaries by nationality indicating that top earners are dispersed throughout the industries.

Viewed from the perspective salary increases, GulfTalent (2016) identifies industries in which salaries increased from 2014 to 2015. The 10 industries ranked from highest to lowest in terms of percentage salary increase are listed below

1. Retail with 6.6 % increase from 2014 to 2015
2. Construction with 6.1 % increase from 2014 to 2015
3. Banking with 6.0 % increase from 2014 to 2015
4. Oil & Gas with 5.9 % increase from 2014 to 2015
5. Telecoms & IT with 5.7 % increase from 2014 to 2015
6. Logistics with 5.5 % increase from 2014 to 2015
7. Real Estate with 5.4 % increase from 2014 to 2015

Table 6.4 Salaries by industry in the year 2008 (table constructed by calculating raw data presented in Government of UAE 2009)

Industrial grouping	Monthly (AED)	Annual (AED)	Annual (US$)	Hours of work
Mining and quarrying	11,227	134,721	36,709	48.2
Financial intermediation	10,961	131,537	35,841	44.1
Electricity, gas, and water supply	10,490	125,882	34,300	47.6
Public administration, defense, and compulsory social security	10,334	124,006	33,789	39.4
Health and social work	6556	78,671	21,436	46.2
Education	6435	77,225	21,042	41.3
Real estate, renting, and business activities	5917	71,007	19,348	47.3
Transport, storage, and communications	4646	55,748	15,190	41.5
Wholesale and retail trade, repair of household goods	4424	53,089	14,466	49.0
Hotels and restaurants	4190	50,280	13,700	50.5
Other community, social, and personal service activities	3741	44,895	12,233	53.8
Manufacturing	3328	39,941	10,883	51.0
Agriculture, hunting, and forestry and fishing	2387	28,642	7804	48.7
Construction	2250	26,998	7356	51.9

8. Health care with 5.2 % increase from 2014 to 2015
9. Education with 4.3 % increase from 2014 to 2015
10. Hospitality with 3.7 % increase from 2014 to 2015.

The combination of data from Table 6.4 and GulfTalent (2016) shows that the lowest paid industry in 2008, construction, received the highest percentage increase in salary in 2015. However, with a mean salary of only US$7356 per month, a 6 % increase would be only around US$441 annually, less than US$37 per month. However, salaries by industry groupings may mask disparities in which annual salary increases are only received by the highest paid employees while the lowest paid employees earn little or no pay raise. However, in a time when the global economy seems to be sluggish, pay increases, even if modest, show stability of the economy and attract migrant workers especially from the region where many economies are in shambles (Raitha 2005).

An examination of salaries by occupation as shown in Table 6.5 helps to explain the salary by industry figures.

For example the top three salary groupings by occupation, *Legislators, Senior Officials and Managers*, *Professionals*, *Technicians*, and *Associate Professionals* are commonly employed in three of the four top earning industries, *Financial Intermediation*, *Electricity, Gas and Water Supply Public Administration*, *Defense* and *Compulsory Social Security*. In addition, the three top earning industries

Table 6.5 Salaries in major occupation groups (table constructed by calculating raw data presented in Government of UAE 2009)

Major occupation group	Monthly (AED)	Annual (AED)	Annual US$	Hours of work
Legislators, senior officials, and managers	13,043	156,519	42,648	199.4
Professionals	11,383	136,600	37,221	181.6
Technicians and associate professionals	6683	80,199	21,853	198.8
Clerks	4639	55,664	15,167	197.3
Service workers, shop, and market sales workers	3227	38,723	10,551	217.9
Plant and machine operators and assemblers	2651	31,812	8668	222.4
Skilled agricultural and fishery workers	2046	24,554	6691	239.4
Craft and related trades workers	1965	23,578	6424	219.4
Not stated	1951	23,409	6379	226.4
Elementary occupations	1634	19,607	5343	213.0

employ large numbers of Emirati employees as advised by AlWaqfi and Forstenlechner (2010).

The reverse is also shown. The lowest paid workers by occupation, *Service Workers, Shop and Market Sales Workers, Plant and Machine Operators and Assemblers, Skilled Agricultural and Fishery Workers, Craft and Related Trades Workers*, and *Elementary Occupations* (domestic and labor) are employed mostly in the lowest paid industries, *Transport, Storage and Communications, Wholesale and Retail Trade, Repair of Household Goods, Hotels and Restaurants, Other Community, Social and Personal Service Activities, Manufacturing, Agriculture, Hunting and Forestry and Fishing*, and *Construction*, several of which also show the lowest percentage increase in salary from 2014 to 2015.

The DEC Study categorized occupation by profession supporting the assertion that salary disparities are being masked by the mean salaries by industry. The four skill levels and corresponding average salaries from the DEC study are listed below

- Senior-professional with mean annual salary of US$39,237
- Semi-professional with mean annual salary of US$22,888
- Clerk/Services/Crafts with mean annual salary of US$6540
- Elementary with mean annual salary of US$4905 (Tong 2010, p. 28).

The average salary earned by employees with the skill levels above corresponds with the salary ranking by occupation in Table 6.5 and corresponds to the expected level of education and experience employees would need to achieve those levels as shown in the next subsection.

Table 6.6 Salaries by education level for the year 2008 (table constructed by calculating raw data presented in Government of UAE 2009)

Education level	Monthly (AED)	Annual (AED)	Annual US$	Hours of work
Doctorate	21,718	260,621	71,014	43
Master	14,300	171,596	46,756	42
Above university diploma	12,301	147,616	40,222	45
University	10,530	126,356	34,429	44
Above secondary and below university	7277	87,324	23,794	45
Secondary	4028	48,334	13,170	48
Preparatory	2304	27,649	7534	50
Read and write	2062	24,742	6742	50
Primary	1960	23,518	6408	51
Illiterate	1855	22,261	6066	56

6.5 Salaries by Education Level

Salaries by education are broken down in detail in Table 6.6 showing a very wide disparity in salaries of employees with high education levels and low education levels.

Table 6.6 illustrates the inverse relationship between working hours and education and salary and education, i.e., workers with lower educational levels work longer hours for less compensation. There seems to be a gradual increase with the greatest increases at the upper levels with an increase in salary of more than an a third between the *Masters* level and the *Doctorate* level of education.

Unskilled labor employed in manual labor earned the least while highly educated and skilled professionals earned the most. As was the case in the study, most of the employees in the UAE labor market were clerks, service workers, craftsmen, and laborers educated at the primary level or less and earning around 24,000 AED (US $6540) annually (Government of UAE 2009).

6.6 Salaries by Age

The slight positive correlation between age and salary in the UAE labor market is most likely because nearly 90 % of the workforce consists of expatriate workers on 1–3 year contracts (Al-Abed et al. 2008). Therefore, when workers tire of a job, become less efficient, or are needed in their home countries, they opt not to renew their contracts. At that point, employers often hire workers at the same level and relatively the same age as the previous employee. Some expatriate employees on one to three year contracts feel unsecure in their jobs because if companies want to cut expenses, they may chose not to renew contracts for highly educated, skilled, and experienced employees at the upper end of the pay scales (Al-Ali 2008). Such companies may opt to employ younger workers who may be less experienced but willing to work for a lower salary (AlWaqfi and Forstenlechner 2014).

Examination of mean salaries by age is not particularly helpful due to the proportionately high number of migrant workers in the UAE workforce and age regulations in UAE labor law. Federal Law No. 7 of 2007 states that UAE nationals with at least 20 years of service may retire at age 48, however, some experts expect the minimum retirement age for UAE nationals to start increasing annually in 2016 eventually settling at age 50 years old (Kapur 2016). Although expatriates do not qualify for retirement benefits in the UAE, the expected retirement age is 60 years old although expatriates may be issued work permits up to a maximum of 65 years old.

A study investigating Emirati job satisfaction found that salaries in the public sector were less related to age than in the private and semi-government sectors. For Emiratis working in the public sector

> job satisfaction criteria related to work environment, salary, benefits, and job security were more important than other job satisfaction criteria, including growth potential and opportunities for advancement. The majority of respondents were willing to work in a single job with little possibility of advancement as long as the salary and workplace conditions were suitable (Daleure and Al Shareef 2015, p. 24).

The same study revealed that with the high degree of saturation in the public sector, promotion was not as frequent as in the other two sectors. Downsizing occurring by attrition did not seem to affect overall job satisfaction and did not seem to prompt Emiratis to seek career advancement opportunities offered in the private sector, at least until after retirement, at which time some participants entered the private sector most commonly in self-employment.

6.7 Salaries by Location

The available studies indicate a positive correlation between mean salaries and population density. Mean salaries in emirates with high population density areas tend to be higher than mean salaries in emirates with lower population density areas. The DEC Study ranked Dubai as having the highest annual salary in 2009 at AED52,800 (US$14,387). Abu Dhabi followed with AED42,000 (US$11,444), Sharjah with AED30,000 (US$8174), Ajman with AED20,400 (US$5559), both Fujairah and Umm Al Quwain with AED18,000 (US$4905), and Ras Al Khaimah with AED13,440 (US$3662) (Tong 2010, p. 7). A shift has taken place with the highest salaries on offer in 2016 available in Abu Dhabi at AED19,349 (US$5272) per month or AED232,188 (US$63,266) per year ("Dubai salary" 2016; "Salary survey" 2016).

Table 6.7 Salaries by economic sector in the year 2008 (table constructed by calculating raw data presented in Government of UAE 2009)

Sector	Monthly (AED)	Annually (AED)	Annually (US$)
Federal government	11,176	134,121	36,545
Local government	9405	112,861	30,752
Joint (semi-government)	7545	90,542	24,670
Foreign	5843	70,116	19,105
Other: not specified	5549	66,599	18,146
Private	3395	40,741	11,101

6.8 Salaries by Economic Sector: Private, Public, Semi-government

Numerous studies exploring the UAE labor market report that the perception among Emiratis is that the public and semi-government sectors offer better compensation packages (Daleure et al. 2014; Sherif 2013). Table 6.7 shows salaries for economic sectors with the salaries for the federal, local, and joint (semi-government) sectors listed separately to show more detail.

As shown, the data in Table 6.7 supports the perception that government sector employees have been offered higher salaries than employees in the private sector. However, the higher salaries offered in government sectors may be more a factor of requiring higher education, more technical skills, and the introduction of policies designed to attract Emiratis into the workforce. The most significant factor reducing the reported salaries for the private sector is most likely inclusion the salaries of domestic workers and laborers in the private sector salary calculations since low skilled and low paid workers comprise the majority of the private sector workforce in the UAE (Willoughby 2005).

6.9 Salaries by Gender

Salaries by gender seem to be counter-intuitive at first glance but reveal very important characteristics about the UAE labor market. The average salary for males in the UAE in 2008 was AED17,073 (US$4652) annually while the average salary for females in the UAE in 2008 was AED47,450 (12,929) annually (Gov of UAE 2009).

There were three reason for these unexpected results. First of all, most (93 %) of the participants in the sample were males and only about 7 % were female. Second, only about 40 % of the males in the sample completed secondary education while double the number (about 80 %) of the females had a secondary education or more. When the male and female salaries were examined for the same educational level, males' salaries were higher than females' salaries. Other studies corroborate that although there are fewer women in the UAE labor market, the women who are in the labor market tend to be more educated than the men (Al Suwaidi 2010; Rutledge et al. 2011).

6.10 Summary

Factors that affect salary in the UAE labor market are summarized below:

- Sizeable variations in compensation existed based demographic factors such as age, gender, education, industries, location, and nationality of workers.
- Length of hours worked were inversely correlated with salaries and education, i.e., workers with higher salaries tended to have higher education levels and shorter working hours.
- Education level was positively correlated with salaries but the degree of correlation depended on the industry and emiratein which the worker was employed.
- Working hours were shorter in the high population density areas of some emirates including Dubai, Abu Dhabi, Sharjah, and Ajman and higher in low population density areas.
- The financial industry appears too ffer the highest salaries while the construction and hospitality industries offer the least. This is partially explained by the required education needed and labor intensity of the sectors.
- More than 75 % or the workers earned less than 40,000 AED (US$10,699) while only 1 % earned more than 40,000 AED.
- Three-fourth of the workforce (76 %) of the workforce consists of workers from the Indian subcontinent.
- Only about 13 % of the workforce had more than a high school education.
- Females had a higher average education level than males, yet earned less than their male counterparts with similar education levels and comprised only 7 % of the total workforce.
- In 2008 around 80 % of the workforce was unskilled labor which dropped off to 72 % in 2009 remaining stable after that. During the same time, salaries for skilled workers increased.
- Construction salaries remained steady at about 800 AED per month up to 2008 then rose slightly in 2009.
- Age was slightly correlated to salary because companies offered slightly higher salaries to new hires over time while the salaries of continuing employees remain stable.

Although not necessarily generalizable, the findings from reports cited in this chapter illustrate the way salary patterns are interrelated in the complex labor market of the UAE. It seems that with Emiratis comprising only about 10 % of the working age population, full employment for Emiratis would be easy to achieve, however, as the findings of the studies presented in this chapter reveal, nearly 80 % of the jobs available in the labor market exist in the labor intensive industries of agriculture, hotels and restaurants, construction and manufacturing, trade and repair services, and logistics (Schiliro 2013).

These are labor intensive industries with few jobs that require a higher education or offer a salary sufficiently high to attract Emiratis. In addition, training programs do not exist for these areas of employment. For example, there are no vocational training programs offered in the country at the postsecondary level in any public or private institutions for skilled vocations such as auto mechanics, auto body repair, detailing or plumbing. The lack of training programs indicates that workers for these and other similar occupations would be hired in as migrant workers with the skills and experience already in place (Weiner 1982; Yousef 2005).

The chapter illustrates the core issue of salaries in the UAE labor market. Desirable salaries are perceived to exist in specific positions or in specific sectors so those areas are the areas in which education is subsidized for Emiratis. Other areas of the economy, namely skilled vocational positions, which have the potential to provide reasonable salaries in other modernized countries, do not have training programs offered in the country. However, with abundant migrant labor available already trained and experienced there appears to be no need to train Emiratis for this type of employment. The difficulty arises in the fact that stiff competition exists for jobs that offer sufficiently high salaries to attract Emiratis, with expatriate workers available that often have more skills, qualifications, and experience than Emirati candidates.

References

Al-Abed, I., Vine, P., Hellyer, P., & Vine, P. (Eds.). (2008). *United Arab Emirates Yearbook: 2008*. London: Trident Press.

Al-Ali, J. (2008). Emiritization: Drawing UAE nationals into their surging economy. *International Journal of Sociology and Social policy, 28*(9/10), 365–379.

Al Suwaidi, J. S. (2010). Introduction: Education and the requirements of the GCC labor market. In *Education and the requirements of the GCC labor market* (pp. 3–8). Abu Dhabi: The Emirates Center for Strategic Studies and Research.

AlWaqfi, M., & Forstenlechner, I. (2010). Stereotyping of citizens in an expatriate-dominated labour market Implications for workforce localisation policy. *Employee Relations, 32*(4), 364–381. doi:10.1108/01425451011051596.

AlWaqfi, M. A., & Forstenlechner, I. (2014). Barriers to Emiratization: The role of policy design and institutional environment in determining the effectiveness of Emiratization. *The International Journal of Human Resource Management, 25*(2), 167–189. doi:10.1080/09585192.2013.826913.

Aydemir, A. B. (2015). Skill-based immigration, economic integration, and economic performance. In K. F. Zimmerman, & A. S. Kritikos (Eds.), *Evidence-based policy making in labor economics The IZA world of labor guide 2015*, (pp. 41–41). London: Bloomsbury.

Constant, A. (2015). Do migrants take the jobs of native workers? In K. F. Zimmerman, & A. S. Kritikos (Eds.), *Evidence-based policy making in labor economics The IZA world of labor guide 2015*, (pp. 38–39). London: Bloomsbury.

Daleure, G., Albon, R. & Hinkston, K. (2014, January). Reshaping attitudes, beliefs, and opinions: The key to Emiratization in the private sector. *Policy Paper No. 8*. Ras Al Khaimah, UAE: Sheikh Saud bin Saqr Al Qasimi Foundation for Policy and Research.

Daleure, G. & Al Shareef, Z. (2015). Exploring under-representation of young Emirati adults in the UAE private sector by examining Emirati job Satisfaction. *Working Paper No. 9*. Ras Al Khaimah: Sheikh Saud Bin Saqr Al Qasimi Foundation for Policy Research.

De Bell Airs, F. (2015). Demography, migration, and the labour market in the UAE. *GLMM - N - No. 7/2015*. Gulf Labour Markets and Migration Center. Available at http://cadmus.eui.eu/bitstream/handle/1814/36375/GLMM_ExpNote_07_2015.pdf?sequence=1

Dubai Salary and Pay Scale. (2016, March 2). *Guide2Dubai Online*. Available at http://www.guide2dubai.com/living/expat-life/dubai-salary-and-pay-scale

Government of the United Arab Emirates [UAE]. (2009). *Employment, wages, and hours worked survey 2008*. Available at www.fcsa.gov.ae

GulfTalent. (2016, March). *Employment and Salary Trends in the Gulf*. Dubai, UAE: GulfTalent. Available at www.gulftalent.com

Hays. (2016). *Salary and employment report: Salaries and trends of the growing GCC market*. Dubai, UAE: Hays Recruiting Experts Worldwide

Kapur, S. (2016, February 24). UAE retirement age set to go up by one year from February-end. *Emirates 24/7 Newspaper* Online. Available at http://www.emirates247.com/news/uae-retirement-age-set-to-go-up-by-one-year-from-february-end-2016-02-24-1.622044

Morgan McKinley. 2016, July). *UAE salary guide 2015*. Dubai, UAE: Morgan McKinley available at https://www.morganmckinley.ae/about/2015-salary-survey-benefits

Raitha, D. (2005, January 1). Workers' remittances: An important and stable source of external development finance. *Economics Seminar Series, no. 9*. (pp. 157–175). St. Cloud State University Repository Open Access. Available at http://repository.stcloudstate.edu/econ_seminars/9

Rutledge, E. J., Al Shamsi, F., Bassioni, Y., & Al Sheikh, H. (2011). Women, labour market nationalisation policies and human resource development in the Arab Gulf States. *Human Resource Development International, 14*(2), 183–193.

Salary survey in Abu Dhabi. (2016). *Salary explorer online database*. Available at http://www.salaryexplorer.com/salary-survey.php

Schiliro, D. (2013, summer). Diversification and development of the United Arab Emirates' economy. *Journal of Applied Economic Sciences*, 228–239.

Sherif, S. (2013). Macroeconomic policy, localization, and reducing unemployment: The crucial human resource issues for the UAE. *Competitiveness Review: An International Business Journal, 23*(2), 158–174.

Tong, Q. (2010, July). *Wages structure in the United Arab Emirates. Working Paper No. 2*. Dubai: Institute for Social & Economic Research.

Weiner, M. (1982). International migration and development: Indians in the Persian Gulf. *Population and Development Review, 8*(1), 1–36.

Willoughby, J. (2005, March). Ambivalent anxieties of the South Asian-Gulf Arab labor exchange. *Department of Economics Working Paper Series, No. 2005-02*. Washington, D.C.: American University. http://www.american.edu/cas/econ/workpap.htm

Yousef, T. (2005). The changing role of labor migration in Arab economic integration. *Policy Seminar on Arab Economic Integration: Challenges and Prospects, February, 23–24, 2005*. Washington, D.C: Center for Contemporary Arab Studies.

Chapter 7
Wage Remittances from the UAE

Abstract This chapter discusses the role of migrant workers from a global perspective, emphasizing that all developed countries import migrant labor as a temporary solution for surplus jobs in the economy or a longer term solution to filling jobs that are below the expectations of the citizenry in terms of compensation or working conditions. Wages and salaries account for most of employers' labor costs and a sizeable portion of the overall cost of operations especially in the service industries. In the modern global economy, citizen workers in most modernized countries compete with migrant workers who enter the country temporarily to work. Salary remittance patterns from the UAE back to the home countries of expatriate workers are examined in terms of the benefits to the economies of the home countries and the loss of GDP to the UAE economy. The chapter concludes with a brief comparison of cost of living estimates exemplifying the ability of expatriate workers, often provided with accommodation, transportation, food, and other benefits in the UAE reducing the overall cost of living. At the same time, the salary remittances uplift the quality of life of the family members left behind in the home country or the lives of the expatriate workers when they repatriate back to their home countries.

Keywords Migrant labor · Expatriate workers · Temporary employees · Wage remittances

7.1 Migrant Labor as a Reality in the Modern Global Economy

Migrant employment can be intra-national, usually from rural areas to urban industrialized areas, or international, usually from developing countries to more developed countries. In their book, *Who needs migrant workers? Labor shortages, immigration, and public policy*, Ruhs and Anderson (2010) thoroughly discuss the role of migrant labor in the modern global economy. Migrant workers are employed into low paying jobs that citizens are unwilling to do or are hired into more

G. Daleure, *Emiratization in the UAE Labor Market*,
DOI 10.1007/978-981-10-2765-9_7

desirable jobs in competition with citizen employees but at a lower wage. The authors imply that this behavior exemplifies the preference of companies to lower costs by employing workers who may be perceived as more easily exploitable than citizen labor.

According to Weiner (1982) migrant workers in developed countries may have a limited education and are hired for positions that the citizen workforce are ether unwilling or unable to fill. However, "a large proportion of the migrants to the Gulf are skilled workers who have entered the modern sectors of the economy in such large numbers that they easily outnumber the local skilled labor force" (p. 2).

In times of prosperity, immigration becomes less restrictive then in times of economic downturn, such as occurred on a global scale in 2008–2009, immigration policies are re-evaluated as increasing citizen workers experience unemployment. Ruhs and Anderson (2010) give examples of tightening immigration policies in the European Union (EU) as the raising of minimum educational qualifications and salary requirements in the UK and blocking previously allowed potential job seekers and allowing only migrants who have received firm job offers to enter Spain. Industries frequently employing migrant labor in Europe include construction, hospitality including food service, general labor, agriculture, and health care which closely mirrors the major industries that employ migrant labor in the UAE as shown in Chap. 6.

Companies in that employ large numbers of migrant workers sometimes rotate the migrant pools as migrants become more aware of the opportunities in the host country and of their own inferior treatment or perceived status in the host countries. MacKinzie and Forde (2009) followed the migrant hiring patterns of companies in the UK discovering that some large companies followed the admission of new entrants into the EU member nations then advertised for workers in those newly admitted countries including Estonia, Lithuania, Latvia, and Poland for temporary contracts. The aim was to secure a temporary labor force at the lowest possible cost with an acceptable work ethic and still remain within the law. However, as noted by Sharma (2006), the longer that migrant workers remain in the host country, the more attached they become to the local environment and the more they become aware of their inferior treatment or status.

> There were diminishing returns associated with employing migrant workers the longer they were established in the labor market and community. It was suggested workers became more demanding as they became more aware of their entitlements and alternative opportunities. Thus, the imperative to move between successive groups of migrant workers was not only driven by quantitative changes in availability but also by qualitative changes in the attributes that management most valued. (Mackinzie and Forde 2009, p. 150)

Chan and Ngai (2009) related ways in which Chinese citizens migrating from rural areas to more developed areas to work in factories and other enterprises faced the same treatment as migrant workers in other countries. Chinese workers from rural areas were housed in dormitory style accommodation in migrant communities provided by the companies for which they work. The condition of the accommodation, i.e., the type of living space, amenities, and community members, combined with efforts of labor organizations have contributed to the formation of a new working class or proletariat and the labor protests starting in 2004.

Sometimes previously untapped citizen groups are targeted as temporary solutions to labor shortages and treated as migrant labor. MacKinzie and Forde (2009) offer two examples. Wives of men working in factories or industrial areas who have previously not worked outside the home may be offered shifts with special timings or part-time working hours while their children are in school to accelerate production or part-time or seasonal work may be offered to young people while still in school to support the regular shift workers.

In the United States (US) the practice of hiring migrant workers from developing countries mostly in South America to serve as in military operations has sparked debate on the status of migrant workers hired by an organization in one country, yet working in another country (Li 2015). In this scenario, the migrant workers performing sensitive missions in a third country, not the country of the employer and not their own country. They have no shared identity with the employing country or the host country in which they are expected to perform their duties. Often times, according to Li, the compensation is so low that the employment is akin to indenturement but with limited options, the migrants accept the posts.

As demonstrated in this subsection, migrant labor provides a lower cost alternative to citizen labor, especially for jobs that citizen workers are unwilling to perform. The next subsection describes the benefits to the migrant workers emphasizing the ability to remit often times large portions of their salaries to their home countries.

7.2 Growing Importance of Wage Remittances to Developing Countries

Raitha (2005) reported that "remittances to low-income countries were larger as a share of GDP and imports than were those to middle income countries. Remittances are also more stable than private capital flows" (p. 157). Remittances may be cash transfers but they may also be in the form of purchases or payments such as gifts of clothing, foodstuff, dowries, real estate purchases, mortgage payments, payment for medical purchases, or contributions to pension funds or investment portfolios, and so on. Sayan (2006) investigated remittance receipts of 12 high remittance countries including Bangladesh, Jordan, Algeria, Jamaica, Lesotho, Pakistan, Turkey, India, Senegal, Dominican Republic, Ivory Coast, and Morocco discovering that for most of the countries, remittances increased as financial conditions in the home countries declined, providing added support for the families of the migrant workers in the home countries while detracting from the economy of the host country.

The wage remittances from workers of some countries account for substantial portions of the Gross National Product (GNP) of their own countries (Amauedo-Dorantes 2015). World Bank reports indicate that remittances to developing countries reached $316 billion in 2009 (Raitha et al. 2010).

7.3 Top Wage Remittance Countries

The top five developing countries receiving remittances worldwide in 2009 were India with US$49 billion, China with US$49 billion, Mexico with US$22 billion, and the Philippines with US$20 billion (Raitha et al. 2010). Kock and Sun (2011) reported leading remittances countries in terms of percentage of GDP in the country of the migrant worker with Lebanon leading with 24 %, Jordan next at 22 %, and the Philippines in third place with 11 %.

According to United Nations figures published for 2013, the top five origin countries for migrant workers to the UAE were India with over 2.8 million workers, Bangladesh with over a million workers, Pakistan with over 950,000 workers, Egypt with over 700,000 workers, and the Philippines with more than 470,000 workers (Malit and AlYouha 2013). Such high remittance figures explain why

> Remittances are now being factored into sovereign ratings in middle-income countries and debt sustainability analysis in low-income countries. Countries are also becoming increasingly aware of the income and wealth of overseas diaspora as potential sources of capital. Some countries are showing interest in financial instruments such as diaspora bonds and securitization of future remittances to raise international capital (Raitha et al. 2010, p. 1).

To understand impact of remittances on the economy of the UAE a brief case study is presented in the next subsection.

7.4 UAE Remittance Outflows: The Case of Pakistan

To demonstrate the significance of remittance outflows on the UAE economy, Pakistan, a county with a sizeable number of migrant workers in the UAE is used as an example. Other countries with high remittance outflows from the UAE include India, the Philippines, Bangledesh, Sri Lanka, Indonesia, Nepal, and China.

World Bank estimates show that worldwide remittances to Pakistan have quadrupled over an 8 year period from 2000 to 2008 to top out at over US$7 billion with remittances from the UAE estimated at nearly US$1.7 billion in 2008 (Kock and Sun 2011, p. 3). The same report states that the remittances to Pakistan from the UAE were second only to remittances from the US which were only slightly more at just over US$1.7 billion. Another study published higher figures for the same period with expatriate remittances from the UAE to Pakistan more than doubling over a 6 year period from US$810 million in 2002 to US$1.902 billion in 2008 (Amjad et al. 2012).

An interesting trend emerges when looking more closely at the remittance patterns. At the same time that the total remittances increased, the percentage of total remittances received in rural areas increased substantially as shown in Table 7.1.

Amjad et al. (2012) theorize that the number of skilled and educated workers from urban areas is remaining steady while increasing numbers of workers from

Table 7.1 Percentages of remittances to urban and rural areas in Pakistan from 1996–97 to 2007–2008 (calculated using raw data published in Amjad et al. 2012)

Year	Urban areas (%)	Rural areas (%)
1996–97	50.7	49.3
2001–02	40.8	59.2
2005–06	33.6	66.4
2007–08	27.6	72.6

rural areas are entering into work abroad. Finding limited economic opportunities, low skilled workers seem to be opting for work abroad, even for a relatively low salary. Kock and Sun (2011) lend support to this theory stating that "given that Pakistan has a relatively large agricultural sector, which employs the majority of the workforce, and many immigrant workers have families or relatives in the rural areas, this result is not surprising" (p. 14).

Table 7.2 shows the number of Pakistani nationals reportedly working abroad and sending remittances back to their country from 2004 to 2012 along with the percentage of total remittances per host country expressed as a percentage of total US dollars.

Table 7.2 shows that the UAE received an increasing percentage of Pakistani workers from 2004 to 2012, at 12.6 and 17.9 %, respectively, with the actual numbers increasing from approximately 738,000 to 1.2 million people, respectively, in the same period. Similar estimates of remittance rates were reported by Naufal and Termos (2009), however, Kock and Sun (2011) reported a slightly

Table 7.2 Expatriate Pakistani workers and remittances from 2004 to 2012 per Host Country (calculated using raw data published in Amjad et al. 2012)

Host country	2004		2009		2012		% of Remittances	
	Persons[a]	%	Persons[a]	%	Persons[a]	%	2004	2009
All countries	3.97	100	5.50	100	6.70	100	100	100
Saudi Arabia	1.10	27.7	1.20	21.8	1.70	25.4	15.1	21.5
United Kingdom	0.80	20.1	1.20	21.8	1.20	17.9	9.0	9.9
USA	0.60	15.1	0.90	16.4	0.90	13.4	31.1	19.9
UAE	0.50	12.6	0.74	13.4	1.20	17.9	17.2	22.9
Canada	0.25	6.3	0.30	5.5	0.30	4.5	1.2	1.2
Oman	0.00	0.0	0.15	2.8	0.20	3.0	2.9	3.2
Kuwait	0.10	2.5	0.15	2.7	0.15	2.2	5.2	5.0
Other countries	0.62	15.5	0.86	15.6	1.05	15.7	18.4	16.3

[a]Expressed in millions

different raking among the top three with remittances from the US at just over US $1.7 billion, followed very closely by the UAE at just under US$1.7 billion, and then Saudi Arabia with just over US$1.6 billion.

The discrepancy in figures illustrates one of the important challenges in collecting field data for any study involving a dynamic population. As a result of the economic downturn starting in 2008, the construction sector slowed down in the UAE. Remittances from the UAE to Pakistan decreased by approximately one third from November 2008 onwards when a large number of Pakistani construction workers relocated from the UAE to Saudi Arabia. Therefore, data collected in different studies at differing points in the transition may explain the variance in reported results.

Although Pakistani remittances were used in the case study, large numbers of migrant workers from the top remitting countries of India, China, and Philippines work in the UAE and all of which reportedly remit more than Pakistani migrants. Although obvious and staggering in terms of sheer monetary value, few studies have been conducted on the effects of remittances on the UAE economy.

7.5 Hawala Transfers Masking Full Impact of Remittances

As huge as they are, figures presented in Table 7.2 are less than the actual remittances as ways exist to transfer money other than bank transfer or through an exchange house. One way to send and receive money off the monitoring grid is called *hawala* transfer or money transfer without money movement. In such transactions people wishing to send money from one country or region to another go to a known hawala agent. They hand over the money to the hawala agents who give them a password. The sender informs the intended recipient of the password by phone who uses the password to obtain the funds in local currency from the corresponding hawala agent in the recipient country. According to one report,

> Hundreds or thousands of these transactions are bundled together over the course of weeks or months with consolidation taking place at various levels. Midlevel hawaladars act as clearing houses for small-scale operators, larger hawaladars act as clearing houses for those in the middle, and so on. In Dubai, at the megalevel, branches of value worth £100,000 are the minimum units of trade in each hawala swap. (Bowers 2009, p. 380)

Hawala transfers are illegal in many countries of the world, yet, as shown in this chapter, the amount of money transferred in this way is astounding. In the UAE, although legal, the hawala industry is regulated and monitored with the money handlers, or hawaladars, "required to register with the Central Bank, keep records of the identities of their customers and alert authorities to any suspicious transactions" Maayeh (2008, p. 1). According to Maayeh, people resort to such means of transfers for four main reasons.

- *Lack of formal financial structures in transfer recipient areas*: When transfers are meant for areas of the world devastated by war or political upheaval, the lack of security discourages the existence of banks and other financial institutions and is sometimes the only way to get funds to the target recipients.
- *Cultural affinity*: Sometimes people making transfers may feel a cultural connection toward the hawala agent or network perceiving it to be more trustworthy than a formal financial institution. This occurs more frequently when the person transferring money is from a rural or isolated area where people are distrustful of strangers or when a sender only speaks a little known language and may not be able to read or write. Illiterate workers or workers with rare languages many not be able to fill out formal transfer forms.
- *Low cost*: The hawala agents operate outside the official financial rules and regulations so that they can arrange transfers for as little as 2 % of the transfer amount, making such transfers attractive to people with small salaries.
- *Anonymity*: Since only a password is exchanged, all parties remain unknown making hawala transfers attractive to workers who are earning money without proper documents or visas. In the UAE, however, as previously mentioned, the industry is monitored so that a record of senders is kept and suspicious activity is reported, thereby reducing the chances of illegal workers using this option to remit funds back to their home countries.

Regardless of the remittance method, the loss to the UAE economy and overall GDP seems to be considerable. Obviously, expatriates working in the UAE do spend a portion of their salaries on living expenses, however, data presented in this subsection show that the losses due to remittance outflows are leaking billions of dirhams of out of the economy.

Emiratization practices in which UAE nationals are given salary stipends or other salary supplements have been criticized as counter-productive to economic growth by some experts. However, hiring UAE nationals, even with high salaries, may be better for the overall economic stability of the country because Emiratis spend all or most of their salaries inside the country contributing to the overall GDP. Using this logic, providing government subsidies or other incentives to private sector companies who hire UAE nationals, may seem counter-intuitive to some, but in reality, this practice may be better for the economy in the long run because it keeps money circulating through the economy rather than exiting from it.

As demonstrated in the previous subsection, even with the downward pressure on salaries, expatriate employees seem to be able to remit huge sums of money back to their home countries. This is because in the local economies of their home countries, economic conditions are such that even a modest or low salary earned in the UAE and remitted may substantially raise the quality of life in the country of remittance. One recruitment expert explained the motivation for working abroad as "always the opportunity of gaining something better or more quickly than you would back home" ("UAE recruiter warns" 2016). It is not uncommon for employees such as watchmen, security officers, service workers, domestic workers, and laborers in the UAE earning around 1000 AED (US$270) per month or less to either completely support their families in their home countries or provide substantial supplements enabling them to build homes, educate their children in private schools, provide seed money to start businesses, or other lifestyle enhancing activities.

To illustrate this point even further, consider the following cost of living comparisons between Dubai and seven comparison countries, including five migrant exporting countries. The raw data used in the comparisons was generated using the cost of living comparison index is available at http://www.numbeo.com/cost-of-living.

Example 1: Karachi, Pakistan

- Consumer Prices in Dubai are 142.82 % higher than in Karachi
- Consumer Prices Including Rent in Dubai are 299.71 % higher than in Karachi
- Rent Prices in Dubai are 1,066.46 % higher than in Karachi
- Restaurant Prices in Dubai are 208.89 % higher than in Karachi
- Groceries Prices in Dubai are 113.13 % higher than in Karachi
- Local Purchasing Power in Dubai is 165.20 % higher than in Karachi

This means that the standard of life maintainable in Dubai with a monthly salary of AED 19247 (US$5252) per month could be maintained in Karachi with Rs140,000 (US$1335).

Example 2: Mumbai, India

- Consumer Prices in Dubai are 143.00 % higher than in Mumbai
- Consumer Prices Including Rent in Dubai are 192.76 % higher than in Mumbai
- Rent Prices in Dubai are 269.81 % higher than in Mumbai
- Restaurant Prices in Dubai are 201.46 % higher than in Mumbai
- Groceries Prices in Dubai are 100.55 % higher than in Mumbai
- Local Purchasing Power in Dubai is 72.57 % higher than in Mumbai

This means that the standard of life maintainable in Dubai with a monthly salary of AED19247 (US$5252) per month could be maintained in Mumbai with Rs120,000 (US$1788).

Example 3: Manila, Philippines

- Consumer Prices in Dubai are 67.90 % higher than in Manila
- Consumer Prices Including Rent in Dubai are 150.06 % higher than in Manila
- Rent Prices in Dubai are 398.00 % higher than in Manila
- Restaurant Prices in Dubai are 152.53 % higher than in Manila
- Groceries Prices in Dubai are 51.69 % higher than in Manila
- Local Purchasing Power in Dubai is 177.93 % higher than in Manila

This means that the standard of life maintainable in Dubai with a monthly salary of AED 19,247 (US$5252) per month could be maintained in Manila with ₱99,000 (US$2114).

Example 4: Jakarta, Indonesia

- Consumer Prices in Dubai are 49.07 % higher than in Jakarta
- Consumer Prices Including Rent in Dubai are 98.84 % higher than in Jakarta
- Rent Prices in Dubai are 201.16 % higher than in Jakarta
- Restaurant Prices in Dubai are 145.63 % higher than in Jakarta
- Groceries Prices in Dubai are 14.48 % higher than in Jakarta
- Local Purchasing Power in Dubai is 193.86 % higher than in Jakarta

This means that the standard of life maintainable in Dubai with a monthly salary of AED 19,247 (US$5252) per month could be maintained in Jakarta with Rp35,000,000 (US$2673).

Example 5: Beijing, China

- Consumer Prices in Dubai are 34.65 % higher than in Beijing
- Consumer Prices Including Rent in Dubai are 54.68 % higher than in Beijing
- Rent Prices in Dubai are 82.26 % higher than in Beijing
- Restaurant Prices in Dubai are 95.22 % higher than in Beijing
- Groceries Prices in Dubai are 8.57 % higher than in Beijing
- Local Purchasing Power in Dubai is 83.48 % higher than in Beijing

This means that the standard of life maintainable in Dubai with a monthly salary of AED19,247 (US$5252) per month could be maintained in Beijing with ¥23,000 (US$3440).

Example 6: New York City, USA

- Consumer Prices in Dubai are 30.69 % lower than in New York, NY
- Consumer Prices Including Rent in Dubai are 27.05 % lower than in New York, NY
- Rent Prices in Dubai are 22.93 % lower than in New York, NY
- Restaurant Prices in Dubai are 35.36 % lower than in New York, NY
- Groceries Prices in Dubai are 42.73 % lower than in New York, NY
- Local Purchasing Power in Dubai is 24.19 % higher than in New York, NY

This means that the standard of life maintainable in Dubai with a monthly salary of AED 19,247 (US$5252) per month could be maintained in New York City with US$7200.

Example 7: London, UK

- Consumer Prices in Dubai are 19.63 % lower than in London
- Consumer Prices Including Rent in Dubai are 12.09 % lower than in London
- Rent Prices in Dubai are 2.81 % lower than in London
- Restaurant Prices in Dubai are 31.03 % lower than in London
- Groceries Prices in Dubai are 8.06 % lower than in London
- Local Purchasing Power in Dubai is 40.89 % higher than in London

This means that the standard of life maintainable in Dubai with a monthly salary of AED 19247 (US$5252) per month could be maintained in London with £4500 (US$6016).

As the examples demonstrate, the differences in cost of living figures in migrant exporting countries prove to be a strong motivator for workers to seek employment in the UAE. In addition, the seven examples support the trend that workers with lower salaries tend to remit a higher percentage of their overall salaries to their home countries than workers with higher salaries.

Workers with higher salaries can afford to have their families accompany them to the UAE and have a high enough salary to afford an acceptable lifestyle inside the UAE. Workers with lower salaries often have accommodation, transportation, and even food included in their overall package and choose to remit most of their salaries back to their families so that their families can improve their living conditions.

The figures presented represent the cost of living for major cities which are most probably much higher than the cost of living in rural areas to which much of the remitted income is sent. Therefore, the remitted income has even more of a positive impact on the living conditions of the migrant workers and their families than is implied in the figures presented.

Emirati employees, on the other hand, face the cost of living increases that occur in the UAE economy which seem to be rising exponentially from year to year. The salary used in the cost of living examples, is an average salary estimate for jobs in which Emiratis are typically employed and significantly higher than target entry level salary of approximately AED 10000 (US$2722) for college educated Emiratis.

7.6 Summary

Migrant workers are employed by all developed countries in the world and usually perform jobs that citizen employees do not want to do often at a wage less than citizen employees would accept. Migrant employees often find the wages and working conditions more appealing than those in their own countries and eagerly accept both the wages and working conditions, especially overtime work, anticipating relocating back to their own countries when the work is completed. Migrant workers often remit portions of their salaries back to their own countries to uplift their quality of life or the quality of life of family members remaining in the home country. Remittances from the UAE are estimate to be in the billions of dirhams each year, however, studies are not available investigating the effects of loss of GDP on the Emirati economy. The governments of some developing countries depend on remittances that national budgets include remittances as a regular component.

References

Amauedo-Dorantes, C. (2015). The good and the bad in remittances flows. In Zimmerman, K. F & Kritikos (Eds.), *Evidence-based policy making in labor economics The IZA world of labor guide 2015*, (pp. 44–45). London: Bloomsbury.

Amjad, R., Arif, G. M., & Irfan, M. (2012). Preliminary study: Explaining the ten-fold increase in remittances to Pakistan 2001–2012. In *PIDE Working Papers 2012* (p. 86). Islamabad: Pakistan Institute of Development Economics.

Bowers, C. (2009). *Hawala, money laundering, and terrorism finance: Macro-lending as an end to illicit remittances* (pp. 379–419). Bowers Macro.

Chan, K. C., & Ngai, P. (2009). The making of a new working class? A study of collective actions of migrant workers in South China. *The China Quarterly, 198*, 287–303.

Kock, U., & Sun, Y. (2011, August). Remittances in Pakistan—Why have they gone up, and why aren't they going down? *Working Paper 11/200*. International Monetary Fund (IMF).

Li, D. (2015). Offshoring the army: Migrant workers and the U.S. military. *UCLA Law Review, 124*, 124–174.

Maayeh, S. (2008, August 26). Hawala money transfers defy regulation efforts. *The National Newspaper Online*. Available at http://www.thenational.ae/news/uae-news/hawala-money-transfers-defy-regulation-efforts

MacKinzie, R., & Forde, C. (2009). The rhetoric of the 'good worker' versus the realities of employers' use and the experiences of migrant workers. *Work, Employment & Society, 23*(1), 124–159. doi:10.1177/0950017008099783.

Malit, F. T. & AlYouha, A. (2013, September 18). Labor migration in the United Arab Emirates: Challenges and responses. *The Online Journal of the Migration Policy Institute*. Available at http://www.migrationpolicy.org/print/4191#.V3-KW3nr0Wc

Naufal, G. S. & Termos, A. (2009, September/December). The responsiveness of remittances to price of oil: The case of the GCC. *OPEC Energy Review*, pp. 184–197

Raitha, D. (2005, January 1). Workers' remittances: An important and stable source of external development finance. *Economics Seminar Series, no. 9*. (pp. 157–175). St. Cloud State University Repository Open Access. Available at http://repository.stcloudstate.edu/econ_seminars/9

Raitha, D., Mohapatra, S., & Silwa, A. (2010, April 23). Outlook for remittances flows 2010–2011. *Migration and Development Brief 12*. World Bank. Available at http://www.worldbank.org/prospects/migrationandremittances

Ruhs, M., & Anderson, B. (2010). Introduction. In M. Ruhs & B. Anderson (Eds.), *Who needs migrant workers? Labor shortages, immigration, and public policy* (pp. 1–14). Oxford: Oxford University Press.

Sayan, S. (2006, February). Business cycles and workers' remittances: how do migrant workers respond to cyclical movements of GDP at home? *IMF Working Paper no. 6/52*. International Monetary Fund [IMF].

Sharma, N. R. (2006). *Home economics: Nationalization of 'migrant workers' in Canada*. Toronto: Toronto University Press.

UAE Recruiter Warns of "Mass Exodus" of Expats Due to High Costs, Lack of Jobs. (2016, June 19). *Arabian business.com*. Available at http://www.arabianbusiness.com/uae-recruiter-warns-of-mass-exodus-of-expats-due-high-costs-lack-of-jobs-635722.html

Weiner, M. (1982). International migration and development: Indians in the Persian Gulf. *Population and Development Review, 8*(1), 1–36.

Chapter 8
Social Transitions Contributing to Emirati Unemployment

Abstract This chapter discusses modern development and the widening generational gaps in Emirati society. Previous chapters have shown that the pre-oil economy extending into the dawn of civilization was based mostly on trade of a single commodity, pearls, and the supporting industries up to the collapse of the natural pearl market. While rapid development vastly improved the living standard of the Emirati people, the accompanying social transitions have brought challenges which will be explained in this chapter. To reshape and develop more productive attitudes, beliefs, and opinions about the modern workplace, policy makers must consider the Emirati society as a whole. This chapter points out measures that can be taken to reduce Emirati employment especially young Emirati adult unemployment. Postsecondary institutions may create initiatives to raise awareness about the skills necessary for success in the modern workplace among students and their families. Labor policy makers could work with private sector employers to improve working conditions for all employees that would ultimately attract more Emirati employees. Private sector work environments could be made more culturally appropriate by giving employees more personal space in mixed-gendered work areas. More flexible work schedules could be adopted in more companies to enable all employees to better balance work and family responsibilities.

Keywords UAE social transitions · Culture studies UAE

8.1 Tribal Nature of Emirati Society

Previous chapters have shown that the pre-oil economy extending into the dawn of written history was based on trade with a single commodity, pearls, serving as the main anchor supporting other traditional industries up to the collapse of the natural pearl market. While rapid development vastly improved the living standard of the Emirati people, the accompanying social transitions brought challenges which are discussed in this chapter.

The tribal nature of Emirati society is in many ways the key to rapid economic development of the country; so understanding the complexities of it is essential for

G. Daleure, *Emiratization in the UAE Labor Market*,
DOI 10.1007/978-981-10-2765-9_8

understanding the issues associated with Emirati unemployment and Emiratization. As shown in previous chapters, the Trucial States, the area now known as the UAE during the colonial period just prior to the oil era, were insulated from the sweeping global changes of the late nineteenth through mid-twentieth centuries by the policies relating to their protectorate status. This isolation, while impeding economic growth, served to preserve the social structure and culture that had existed for many centuries. Modern Emirati society is based on tribal roots, yet has evolved to meet the challenges of the twenty-first century.

8.2 Emirati Society Transitioning into the Present

Most Emiratis identify themselves with a particular family group and can trace their male lineage several generations into the past. Each group of extended families is expected to support each other socially and economically. Up to the present day, males in the family are perceived to

> have a corporate responsibility to provide support and protection. The individual head of the family [consisting of himself, wife and children] is traditionally bound by inescapable obligations of mutual assistance and a concept of joined honor to his immediate blood relatives—father, brothers, paternal uncles, cousins (Heard-Bey 2001, pp. 98–99).

In the pre-nationalization era, elder males were effectively the family leaders with younger males serving important familial functions. Women were active in their own spheres contributing to tribal affairs effectively, yet "mostly from behind the scenes" (AlSayegh 2001, p. 19). In contemporary Emirati society, males are held legally and financially responsible for their families. Family members include wives, children, and aging or elderly parents as well as extended family members including grandparents, unmarried females, ill or infirm relatives, and others. In recent years, older females, typically older sisters or aunts, usually with their own incomes, have been serving as guardians for their younger family members when their parents pass on or become advanced in age (Daleure et al. 2014).

8.2.1 Demographic and Family Structure Transitions

In a recent study population study, *Demography of the Arab work and Middle East from the 1950s to the 2000s: A Survey of Changes and Statistical Assessment*, Tabutin and Schoumaker (2005) describe the demographic shifts that occurred in the MENA region in the latter half of the last century. In the period corresponding to the pre-nationalization era, large families were desired as child mortality by age 4 was high at around 12 % and the average life expectancy was low at approximately 40 years old. Early marriage was encouraged at the onset of puberty with girls as young as 12 years old marrying boys as young as 17 years old. Over the last two decades, marriage ages for females shifted almost a decade to allow time for many females to earn a postsecondary degree. Family sizes have remained relatively high although the rate of children per woman has decreased due to drastically reduced child and infant mortality.

In the pre-nationalization days, divorce was not considered a shame and multiple remarriages after divorce were common for both men and women. Wealthy men often married more than one wife, as was and still is allowed by custom and religion. Assuring that all women were married meant that they would be protected and provided for and that children would be born to maintain or even increase the size of the family group. In the pre-nationalization structure, the woman's place in society was clearly defined by her marriage. Family preferences in marriages favored paternal cousins—son and daughter of two brothers—if available. If not available, maternal first cousins or other extended family members were acceptable. If no suitable family member was available, a marriage could be arranged outside the family especially if there was a commercial or geographic tie between the families. Brides left their family homes to live with their husbands' families often caring for the elderly female relatives of their husbands' family. Commonly, newly married couples occupied in a separate section of a dwelling housing many branches of the husbands' extended families (AlSayegh 2012; Heard-Bey 2001).

Age was respected with older men and women often consulted for their opinions on personal, family, and external matters. Younger unmarried women generally stayed at home unless suitably accompanied. In recent years, however, married women have begun chaperoning younger unmarried sisters on outings, in contrast to the experience of women in past generations (Crabtree 2007; Schvaneveldt et al. 2005).

Experts agree that family units (extended, nuclear, and those with multiple branches) are still considered the basis of Emirati society. Marriage continues to be an expectation for Emirati males and females with marriage and having children soon after marriage a desirable outcome. However, marriage is coming later in life particularly for Emirati females and the average number of children born per woman is decreasing (Tabutin and Schoumaker 2005). In Crabtree's (2007) study, students who were unmarried at 22–24 years old had mothers who had married at 13–15 years old and students who had 8 or 9 siblings anticipated having 5 or less children when they eventually marry.

8.2.2 Transitions in Education and Emirati Young Adult Perceptions

Education was important in the pre-nationalization days and is seen by Emirati society as essential in the modern life for both males and females. In the pre-national period, children were taught informally by the local religious leaders in the mosques, under trees, or in private homes (Daleure et al. 2014). The Emirati perspective of the importance of education was confirmed during the nationalization process when education was made compulsory for both boys and girls and free of charge into tertiary education for qualifying nationals of both genders. However, as reported by Ridge (2009) and supported by Zuraik (2005) in a study funded by the UNESCO, family educational expectations for males tend to be lower than females, particularly in families with parents who have less than secondary education.

Females, on the other hand, have been encouraged to study at least up to the point of marriage offers. As a result, females outnumber males more than 2–1 in tertiary education. College-educated Emirati females expressed concern and frustration that males are not continuing their tertiary education. The young Emirati women feared that males may prefer to have wives that have the same or less education than the males have obtained (Hassane and Abdullah 2011).

In a study investigating the factors influencing the behaviors and attitudes of young Emirati adults, Simadi and Kamali (2004) report that only religion outweighed family expectations as the most important factor influencing behaviors of young adult Emirati males and females. Another study investigated the specific social issues concerning Emirati university students with the top concerns listed as road accidents (86 %), smoking (85 %), high divorce rates (84 %), and among the Emirati females, high school dropout rates (80 %) of Emirati males (Hassane and Abdullah 2011).

These studies reflect the transitioning concerns of young adult Emiratis who are personally affected by the large number of traffic fatalities each year, increasing cases of smoking related illnesses among their family members, and rising divorce rates among their friends, parents, or other relatives. Emirati females were particularly concerned about high secondary and tertiary attrition rates among Emirati males because males persist to the post-secondary level less than half as frequently as females (Ridge 2010). In a society where males are socially and financially responsible for their families, some Emirati females may perceive that lower numbers of similarly educated Emirati males may limit their marriage prospects.

AlSayegh (2001), Crabtree (2007), and Schvaneveldt et al. (2005) reported social concerns that the relatively relaxed standards of personal freedom experienced by some Emirati males may prevent them from developing the discipline and strength in character needed to meet the cultural expectations of becoming the heads of households and community leaders. Ridge (2010) concurred recommending that parents demand “higher standards from their [male] children” (p. 29).

8.2.3 Compulsory National Service for Emirati Males

The recent law mandating national service may be one way to assure that Emirati youth are prepared to meet society’s social and vocational expectations. According to Federal Law No. 6 for 2014, Emirati males from age 18–30 years old who finish high school must serve for 12 months, increased from the 9 months originally specified in 2014, while Emirati males who have not finished high school must serve for 2 years (UAE National Service 2016). National Service for Emirati females is optional and requires guardian’s consent (Government of UAE 2015).

Amna Rashid Al Yamahi, head of the strategy section at the strategic planning department of the UAE Armed Forces, reports that

> While some of today's youths may be directionless, the service will give them a sense of purpose and identity. It would teach them valuable skills, both vocational and social.... The National Service is a genuine step towards raising the awareness of Emirati youth to national principles, preserving the country's achievements and strengthening patriotism, as well as boosting discipline (UAE National Service 2015, paras 2 and 7).

Reports indicate that large numbers of Emiratis in the non-required age group of 30–40 years old have voluntarily registered for National Service after a 15-week volunteer program was announced. The large number of volunteers, according to the National Service and Reserve Authority, signifies that Emiratis of all ages are willing to "volunteer to serve the country with pride and without any hesitation" (Emiratis Voluntarily Join 2016).

8.3 Multilayer Generational Gap

The Oxford online dictionary defines generational gap as "drastic changes that occur in a time range that is roughly the life expectancy of a person resulting in generational miscommunications and misunderstandings." The social structure in the UAE and in other Gulf Cooperation Council (GCC) countries described in detail in the preceding section, is based on tribal familial affiliations, in which "opinions and viewpoints of family elders heavily influence the decisions of younger Emiratis" (AlAbed et al. 2008).

At the same time, the recent rapid and progressive economic developments in the region "caused social transitions in which each consecutive generation was raised with a vastly different set of social circumstances than the preceding generation" (Daleure et al. 2014, p. 3). The differences in experiences have led to the creation of a generational gap between the economic, social, educational, and work experiences of young adults and those of their parents and grandparents.

This section briefly summarizes the important elements of specific previously mentioned contexts and links the effects of each context to the individual in the corresponding generation:

- Elder Adults (older than 65 years old)—likely retired, memories of life before nationalization
- Prime-Age adults (from 46 to 65 years old)—prime of life to retirement, likely to have grandchildren
- Mature adults (from 26 to 45 years old)—completed education, likely working, likely married and raising a family
- Young adults (from 18 to 25 years old)—college-aged generation and first time job seekers.
- Youth (less than 18 years old)—not yet graduated from high school.

The following subsections describe each cohort in more detail.

8.3.1 *Elder Adults (Older Than 65 Years Old)*

People in the elder adult generation were born before the 1950s. They lived well before nationalization and experienced a lifestyle reflecting the harsh realities of life at that time. In their youth, many elder adults lived a semi-transitory life migrating seasonally from the interior to the coast with their families. As children and young adults, they did not have modern conveniences that were becoming commonplace in the rest of the world at the time such as air conditioners, cars, televisions, and refrigerators. Relatively few products were available in the markets (Heard-Bey 2001).

The region lacked most modern social and physical infrastructures including electricity and water piped to individual homes. Most business was done either by trading in kind or using Indian rupees. Most people had little or no formal education, although many received an informal basic education by the local religious leaders or volunteers. The limited available modern healthcare services were provided mainly by the visiting missionaries.

Most people subsisted through fishing, date cultivation, and animal husbandry not unlike their predecessors throughout the centuries (Alsayegh 2001). Immediately following unification, the nation's leadership began the process of building the country's modern physical and social infrastructure (Alabed et al. 2008). Elder adults experienced the gradual improvement of living standards over time.

8.3.2 *Prime-Age Adults (from 46 to 65 Years Old)*

Prime-aged adults were born in the 1950s and 1960s when air concessions and petrol exploration concessions enabled the leaders to take the first steps toward modernization. As the economy started to respond to the modest injection of wealth, new products started to be available in local markets. Some Emirati young people traveled abroad to study and for training. European and American business people began to trickle in usually to fill a temporary post or station. Local merchants begin to form groups to combine their resources to sponsor community projects such as forming the first utility company to provide electricity residents of Dubai (Alsayegh 2012).

8.3.3 *Mature Adults (from 26 to 45 Years Old)*

Mature adults were born in the post-unification period of the 1970s to the 1980s. The post-unification period was characterized by construction and expansion. Modern comforts and devices were introduced and contact with the outside world was re-established (Daleure et al. 2014a). Mature adults did not experience the relatively harsher living conditions of their parents' generation. On the contrary, they grew up in a time of relative ease as people began settling in urban areas to take advantage of the benefits of being a citizen of the UAE.

Markets were rapidly filled with products from all over the world. Municipal electricity and water were made available to people living in the expanding urban centers. Communications systems were developed and expanded to enable landline phone service and cable television. People started to buy cars, paved roads were built, and high rise business and residential towers were constructed (Alsayegh 2001).

The benefits of being an Emirati citizen included receiving basic social services such as education and health care available at little or no cost to Emiratis (Alabed et al. 2008). Near the end of this period, a sedentary lifestyle was well established with Emiratis driving cars, shopping in supermarkets and grocery stores rather than open air markets, and learning how to use newly available technology in everyday life (Heard-Bey 2001). During this period, jobs were plentiful and required only a basic education as

> A wave of Emiratis, educated at a basic level in the fledgling educational system, eagerly left school before graduating to accept public sector posts that offered relatively short working hours (7:30 a.m. to 2:00 p.m.), generous salary and benefits packages, and other incentives (Daleure et al. 2014a, b).

Emiratis joined the police or military receiving similarly high salaries and attractive benefits packages. Even after absorbing as many Emiratis as were available, expatriate labor was needed at every skill and education level to facilitate development efforts at the increasing pace of economic expansion (Alabed et al. 2008; Al-Ali 2013; Alsayegh 2001; Forstenlechner and Rutledge 2011).

8.3.4 *Young Adults (from 18 to 25 Years Old)*

Young adults were born in the late 1980s up through the 1990s. As they grew up they experienced both the benefits and the side effects of rapid development. Changes in lifestyle, nutrition, and improved health care enabled the population to increase rapidly after nationalization. Despite a family structure shift from extended to nuclear families, later marriages for women, and a decrease in births per woman, family sizes continued to increase (Tabutin and Schoumaker 2005). In 2005 a national census was held revealing that 51 % of the Emirati population was age 15 or younger (Sherif 2013).

By the early 2000s, Emiratis had embraced technology. Internet connectivity, personal computers, and mobile phones were an important part of the UAE's social structure and growing economy (AlAbed et al. 2008). In the 1980s public postsecondary institutions were created to educate students graduating high school, many of which were the first in their families to do so. As the students graduated, they expected to find jobs but buy this time the public sector was becoming saturated. In 2002, the federal government approved a plan to Emiratize federal government jobs to absorb unemployed Emirati men and women, many of whom had college degrees, and to decrease dependence on foreign workers (Al-Ali 2013).

Emirati women, educated and ready to contribute to the development of the country, entered the workforce in large numbers by 2010 (Daleure et al. 2014a). By 2011 women made up "two-thirds of the government sector workers and 20 % of the diplomatic corps" (Al-Ali 2013, p. 32). Women were working in the police, military, special forces, customs, municipalities, and were members of the Federal National Council (FNC). Public sector employment was, and still is, especially appealing to Emirati women who often prefer working in "women's sections" separated from men and desired shorter working hours to have more time to take care of children and family matters (Shallal 2011).

Young adult males, facing increased by family pressure to marry after entering the workforce, began to seek employment in occupations that they perceive as high paying rather than personally suitable or interesting (Daleure et al. 2014a). Marriage ages in the young adult generation increased on average from about 15 years old to about 23 years old for women and from about 20 years old to 25 years old for men so that young men could finish their college education and obtain their first job (Tabutin and Schoumaker 2005). In contrast, many young women opted to marry as soon as a suitable man proposed. As a result, some young men, in preparation for marriage, borrowed large sums of money to pay for wedding parties, bride dowries, honeymoon trips, and other preparations satisfying the social and familial expectations, yet leaving them heavily in debt (Al-Ali 2013).

8.3.5 Youth (Less Than 18 Years Old)

Emirati youth are people born after the year 2000. Many Emirati youths have attended private school with many of their subjects delivered in English, had foreign nannies or caregivers, and have been connected to the Internet since they were small children. With the UAE's growing international exposure came the fear that traditional and cultural values were eroding. Allagui and Breslow (2011) reported that the majority (67 %) of 18-year-old Emiratis surveyed spent more time on the Internet chatting with friends than visiting family members. In the same study, the increased use of English language in popular social media websites was blamed for the decreasing proficiency in Arabic language exhibited by Emirati youth. To communicate on the Internet, many young Emiratis started using a hybrid language "Arabish"—Arabic words written using English letters and special characters—rather than Arabic (Hassane and Abdullah 2011).

8.4 Summary

This chapter illustrates the multidimensional aspects of the generational gap. The educational level progresses from informal learning for elderly adults, basic education for most mature adults, to federally funded postsecondary education in English for young adults and youth. The livelihood of the elders was based around agrarian activities in which both males and females participated. Mature adults worked mainly in the public sector with salaries which were substantial enough to allow women to manage the households without working outside the home.

With added financial pressures associated with a modern lifestyle, an increasing number of the young adults are choosing jobs for anticipated salaries rather than matching their aptitudes, skills, and interests and the income contribution of young adult females is increasing being considered as required to sustain the lifestyle that has become expected in Emirati society. It is expected that as more Emiratis with postsecondary education become parents, they will be able to support their own children to successfully achieve higher educations as well (Devereau 2015).

References

AlAbed, I., Vine, P., Hellyer, P., & Vine, P. (Eds.). (2008). *United Arab Emirates Yearbook: 2008*. London: Trident Press.

Al-Ali, J. (2013). *Localizing the GCC workforce: A study and a manual for employers, employees, and job seekers*. Dubai: Masar Printing and Publishing.

AlSayegh, F. (2001). Women and economic changes in the Arab Gulf: The case of the United Arab Emirates. *Digest of Middle East Studies (DOMES), 10*(2), 17–29.

AlSayegh, F. (2012). Women of the Gulf during the first half of the twentieth century: A comparative study of American missionary archives and local memory. In A. E. Sonbol (Ed.), *Gulf women* (pp. 241–276). Qatar: Bloomsbury Qatar Foundation Publishing.

Allagui, I., & Breslow, H. (2011). The internet, fixity, and flow: Challenges to the articulation of an imagined community. In R. Fisher & D. Riha (Eds.), *New media and the politics of online communities*. Oxford: Inter-Disciplinary Press.

Crabtree, A. (2007). Culture, gender and the influence of social change amongst Emirati families in the United Arab Emirates. *Journal of Comparative Family Studies, 38*(4), 575–788.

Daleure, G., Albon, R., & Hinkston, K. (2014a, January). Reshaping attitudes, beliefs, and opinions: The key to Emiratization in the private sector. In *Policy Paper No. 8*. Ras Al Khaimah, UAE: Sheikh Saud bin Saqr Al Qasimi Foundation for Policy and Research.

Daleure, G., Kane, P. Abdalla, H., Rashid, M., Alaskar, S., Ibrahim, M., et al. (2014b). Using "holistic sustainability" to preserve unique cultural identity while participating in the contemporary global economic and social environment: the case of the United Arab Emirates. In *Proceedings of the 4th annual leadership in learning in the asian century conference*. Penang, Malaysia: ELLTA society.

Devereau, P. J. (2015). Intergenerational return to human capital. In K. F. Zimmerman and A. S. Kritikos (Eds.), *Evidence-based policy making in labor economics The IZA world of labor guide 2015*, (pp. 194–195). London: Bloomsbury.

Emiratis Voluntarily Join National Service. (2016, July 11). *UAE Interact Website*. Available at http://www.uaeinteract.com/docs/Emiratis_voluntarily_join_national_service/76320.htm

Forstenlechner, I., & Rutledge, E. J. (2011). The GCC's "demographic imbalance": Perceptions, realities and policy options. *Middle East Policy, 18*(4), 25–43.

Government of the United Arab Emirates. (2015, February 25). *Circular No. (09) of 2015 AD on Instructions of employees joining to the national service*. Abu Dhabi, UAE: United Arab Emirates Federal Authority for Government Human Resources Director General.

Hassane, S., & Abdullah, A. (2011, March). Exploring the most prevalent social problems in the United Arab Emirates. *International Journal of Academic Research, 3*(2). Retrieved from http://www.ijar.lit.az/en.php?go=march2011

Heard-Bey, F. (2001). The tribal society of the UAE and its traditional economy. In I. Al-Abed & P. Hellyer (Eds.), *United Arab Emirates: A new perspective* (pp. 98–116). London: Trident Press.

Ridge, N. (2009). The hidden gender gap in education in the UAE. *Policy Brief no 6*. Dubai: Dubai School of Government.

Ridge, N. (2010, May). Teacher quality, gender, and nationality in the United Arab Emirates: A crisis for boys. *Working Paper Series 10-06*, Dubai: Dubai School of Government.

Shallal, M. (2011). Job satisfaction among women in the United Arab Emirates. *Journal of International Women's Studies, 12*(3), 114–134.

Schvaneveldt, P., Kerpelman, J., & Schevaneveldt, J. (2005). Generational and cultural changes in family life in the United Arab Emirates: A comparison of mothers and daughters. *Journal of Comparative Family Studies, 36*(1), 77–92.

Sherif, S. (2013). Macroeconomic policy, localization, and reducing unemployment: The crucial human resource issues for the UAE. *Competitiveness Review: An International Business Journal, 23*(2), 158–174.

Simadi, F. A., & Kamali, M. A. (2004). Assessing the values structure among United Arab Emirates University students. Social behavior and personality: *An International Journal, 32*(1), 19+. Retrieved from http://www.questia.com

Tabutin, D., & Schoumaker, B. (2005). The demography of the Arab World and the Middle East from the 1950s to the 2000s: A survey of change and a statistical assessment. *Population, 60* (5/6), 505–523.

UAE National Service Draft Strategy Announced. (2015, January 6). *UAE Interact Website*. Available at http://www.uaeinteract.com/docs/UAE_National_Service_draft_strategy_announced/65804.htm

UAE Extends National Military Service Extended to 12 Months. (2016, March 8). *UAE Interact Website* available at http://www.uaeinteract.com/docs/UAE_extends_national_military_service_extended_to_12_months/74397.htm

Zuraik, E. (2005). A study of success and failure patterns in the public high schools of the Emirate of Sharjah in the UAE. *UNESCO Report*. Sharjah, UAE: UNESCO. (Arabic and English)

Chapter 9
Education, the Work Force, and Emiratization

Abstract After nationalization, Emiratis migrated from rural areas to cities settling into a more stationary lifestyle including sending their children to school. Recognizing the need for a highly educated and technologically sophisticated UAE national workforce, the government approved laws, and policies to guarantee equal educational opportunities to UAE national males and females and to encourage UAE nationals to develop themselves to their fullest potential. Education is mandatory up through the primary grades and free of charge to Emiratis up to the completion of high school. After graduation, UAE nationals who qualify academically are guaranteed access free of charge to up to 6 years of postsecondary education at any of the federally funded institutions. Scholarships are available to qualifying UAE nationals who wish to study abroad in specialty areas that are not available in the UAE. Few other countries encourage and subsidize postsecondary education to the extent of the UAE.

Keywords Education in UAE · Postsecondary education in UAE · Higher education in UAE

9.1 Creating an Educational System

In the days before nationalization, few people were able to study abroad and most education in the Trucial States, area by which the UAE was known before nationalization, was informal and consisted mostly of learning to read in Arabic and to recite the Holy Quran (Al-Sayegh 2012; El-Saadi 2012) In the early 1900s, in the days of the last pearling boom, a few schools were set up by wealthy business people in Dubai and Sharjah. In 1903 pearl merchants founded the Taimiyyah School in which students attended free of charge taught by teachers from the community using traditional methods.

A few year later, the Al-Ahmadiyyah school was established showing an early type of private modern education. Students of the Al-Ahmadiyyah school paid a

G. Daleure, *Emiratization in the UAE Labor Market*,
DOI 10.1007/978-981-10-2765-9_9

small fee to attend, however, the school provided desks and instructional materials and employed foreign teachers (Al-Sayegh 1998).

In a study examining life in the UAE prior to nationalization, 50 elderly Emiratis recounted their early life experiences to members of a student research team. Nearly half (22 out of 50) of the participants recalled their early educational experiences as their most cherished memories as related by this excerpt from the study presenting results of a thematic analysis on educational experiences at the time.

> Schools that offered good education, appropriate books, and high-quality teachers were hard to find (EN1). He wasn't in any school or kindergarten, he used to go to the masjid [mosque] to learn Quran, math, Arabic, how to read and write, because there wasn't any kind of school except for the Mutawaa. Al Mutawaa is a person who teaches the children several subjects in a mosque or under trees. He said that there were some women volunteers who were teaching girls in the homes of the girls (EN11).

> The class was usually after Asr [afternoon prayer] and we'd make a big circle and everyone learned how to read correctly. If the teacher found a mistake she would stop you and correct you. I memorized two chapters of Quran. We relied on our parents' experience to know more than that. Respect came first, you have to respect everyone, [you have to know] how to be humble and honest and that we got from hearing stories from others. They taught us important lessons (EN19) (Daleure et al. 2014, p. 22).

These examples illustrate the social importance placed on education and the need to "initiate educational development aimed at improving social awareness" (Al-Sayegh 1998, p. 91). However, the decline of the natural pearl market and economic depression forced the early schools to close, leaving the only the informal option for most of the people of the region.

Since there was no formal educational system at nationalization, the Kuwaiti government assisted in setting up schools which were staffed with teachers mostly from Egypt and the Levant. After nationalization, Emiratis migrated from rural areas to cities settling into a more stationary lifestyle to reap the benefits of citizenry including enrolling their children in school. Recognizing the need for a highly educated and technologically sophisticated UAE national workforce, the government approved laws and policies to guarantee educational opportunities to UAE national males and females and to encourage all UAE nationals to develop themselves to their fullest potential. To accomplish this goal, the government made education compulsory up through grade 10 and free of charge to Emiratis up to the completion of high school.

After graduation, UAE nationals who qualify academically are guaranteed access free of charge to up to 6 years of postsecondary education at any of the federal postsecondary institutions including the Higher Colleges of Technology (HCT), Zayed University (ZU), and United Arab Emirates University (UAEU). Scholarships are available to qualifying UAE nationals who wish to study abroad in specialty areas that are not available inside the country (Al-Abed et al. 2008).

By 2005 the leadership of the UAE expected Emirati youth to complete high school as a minimum educational level to gain employment with a college degree desired. However, even with a college education, some Emirati young adults remain unemployed (Sherif 2013).

9.2 Factors for Early Exit from the Educational System

In a study conducted by the United Nations Educational, Scientific, and Cultural Organization (UNESCO) in government secondary schools in the emirate of Sharjah, Zuraik (2005) found that there were *push* and *pull* factors that detracted from the primary and secondary school experience of Emirati youth and that these factors differed between genders. Males were "pulled into" the labor market (particularly police and/or military) upon completion of high school or earlier. Some males were expected to contribute to the support of their family as soon as possible even if it meant leaving school. Zuraik found a link between students with parents with only informal education and students who did not believe that 12 years of formal education was a necessary preparation to get a good job.

In the same study, the influence of peer groups or family circumstance was found to dissuade students from completing high school. The factors that "pulled" females from school were usually associated with marriage, caring for younger siblings, or other family-related circumstances. Factors that "pushed" both males and females toward early school departure were related to the nature of instruction in schools. In some schools, traditional rote instruction and memorization served to demotivate and disinterest students. In addition students reported a general perception that their teachers did not care about them as individuals, and conducted poorly executed lessons that bored or confused students making attending school less attractive. Similar issues were reported in some private schools.

Ridge (2009) studied government schools in the emirate of Ras Al Khaimah and found similar issues in boys' schools but much better quality of education in girls' schools. Ridge found that in boys' schools, nearly all teachers and administrators were expatriates from other Arab countries or the Indian subcontinent and generally poorly paid. In some classrooms, student management was an issue and the premises were littered, dingy, and run down. In the girls' schools, the environment was much better. More of the teachers and administrators were Emiratis who received higher salaries than expatriates. The Emirati teachers spent some of their own money to make the classrooms more attractive and more often purchased special supplies for their own classrooms. The premises of girls' schools were cleaner, decorated, and pleasant. Classroom management was more effective and the students were less challenging to the teachers.

Issues such as the ones reported in these two studies have prompted the leadership of the country to revamp in the primary and secondary educational system with the updated strategic initiates released in 2010 with 10 strategic objectives organized under five broad themes (Adapted from *The Ministry of Education Strategy 2010–2020*, Government of the UAE 2010, p. 2).

Theme 1: Student Outcomes

- Objective 1: Ensure high-quality curriculum is in place so that students are best prepared for the knowledge economy
- Objective 2: Ensure all students receive excellent teaching from all education staff.

Theme 2: Student School Life

- Objective 3: Develop primary and secondary education across the UAE and minimize dropouts
- Objective 4: Ensure excellent learning environment and tools, to ensure that students' needs are met.

Theme 3: Student Equality

- Objective 5: Install a harmonized assessment on federal level and ensure that students with special needs receive extra and individualized support to integrate them into the educational system
- Objective 6: Ensure an affordable, high-quality standard of Public and Private education is accessible to all students.

Theme 4: Student Citizens

- Objective 7: Promote National Identity and develop the sense of belonging of students
- Objective 8: Foster the society's direct contribution to the school environment.

Theme 5: Administrative Effectiveness

- Objective 9: Ensure that all support services in Zones are conducted in a timely and efficient way
- Objective 10: Ensure that all support services in the Ministry are conducted 10 in a timely and efficient way.

The *Educational Strategy 2010–2020* document affirmed the importance of roles of the major stakeholder groups including students, teachers, parents, and the community, calling on all to contribute to establish a successful educational system. Further improvements were unfolding as preparation of this book was taking place including establishing the Emirates Foundation for Schools which will be run by an independent board of directors and will be accountable to the government for achieving national targets in education and restructuring of the Ministry of Education to have strategic oversight over nurseries and postgraduate institutes (Kapur 2016).

9.3 Postsecondary Education Overview

Demand for postsecondary education has been increasing since the 1990s leading to an increase in the establishment of both public and private postsecondary institutions. Rensimer (2015) attributes the high demand to

> High birth rates among Gulf nationals, staggering inbound migration to meet labor needs, and the increased participation of Gulf women in higher education – all of which have placed greater pressure on institutions and policymakers to accommodate growing populations in higher education (p. 1).

The unique development pattern of the UAE, i.e., isolation up to the mid-1960s followed by rapid growth and development over a period of about 40 years, led to economic benefits and social consequences, both of which have had their effects on higher education in the UAE (Wagie and Fox 2005).

To prepare Emiratis to enter the rapidly changing workforce, the leadership established federally funded colleges and universities in which eligible Emiratis attend free of charge. The first federally funded postsecondary institution, United Arab Emirates University (UAEU) opened in Al Ain in 1977. The first campus of the Higher Colleges of Technology (HCT) opened in the late 1980s and by the mid-2000s the system grew to 17 men's and women's campuses around the country. Zayed University (ZU) for women opened in 1998 with a campus in Abu Dhabi and campus in Dubai (Al-Abed et al. 2008). In 2010, ZU began operating classes in Abu Dhabi for men in 2009 conducted in a separate building and evening classes for men in Dubai in 2010 (Swan 2010).

English is used as the medium of instruction for the federally funded postsecondary institutions because English fluency is considered important for Emirati graduates given the multinational labor market and global economy even though students' native language is Arabic and most public school instruction is delivered in Arabic (Wagie and Fox 2005). Both HCT and ZU are organized and run based on the North American model and the majority of instructors are from English-speaking countries (Al-Abed et al. 2008).

Federally funded institutions admitting only Emirati students exist side by side with an increasing number of private postsecondary institutions and institutions established by the governments of the individual emirates. The commercialization of education has led to a rapid increase in private institutions offering degree programs. The number increased from handful in 1990 to over 109 accredited institutions providing degree programs to approximately 150,000 students in 2015. With commercialization of education comes concerns that "many commercial providers tend to prioritize the affordability and convenience over educational quality and may engage in a range of questionable practices aimed at capitalizing on student demand" (Rensimer 2015, p. 2).

Especially concerning for some are postsecondary institutions in the free zones of Dubai and Ras Al Khaimah which allow institutions to exist inside the country without being accredited by the national accreditation body. When seeking educational equivalencies required to work in government jobs and in many private sector jobs, degree documents from unaccredited institutions within free zones must be approved by the authorities.

Studies show that the most common way for Emirati students to choose their postsecondary educational institutions is by word of mouth rather than individual exploration such as visiting the institution or reading reviews. The majority of Emirati students who qualify choose to go to the federally funded postsecondary institutions because they are free of charge and because the programs are considered to be of good quality. Interestingly, some Emirati parents who are wealthy enough to pay for their children to attend private postsecondary institutions, opt instead for them to attend public postsecondary institutions precisely *because they do not pay*. Emiratis may perceive that in institutions in which students pay tuition, administrators and teachers may lower standards to retain students. However, in public postsecondary institutions the perception is that students will learn more because the teachers are paid and monitored by the government so students are less likely to get grades that are not earned (Daleure 2011; Wagie and Fox 2005). Females preferred public postsecondary institutions because they have separate campuses for males and females (Daleure 2005).

9.3.1 Gender Imbalance in Postsecondary Education

By the mid-2000s, female Emiratis attending postsecondary education outnumbered males by two-thirds, approximately 35 and 65 %, respectively (Ridge 2010). As previously mentioned, males sometimes experience social and economic pressure to discontinue postsecondary education and start working. Females are often under less pressure from their families than males to work and are able to continue their studies to a higher level before considering employment options (Daleure 2005).

A study investigating Emirati male persistence into postsecondary education (Daleure 2011) indicated that the participants, Emirati males attending public postsecondary institutions in the Northern Emirates, who persisted into postsecondary education, either working or not working, had the support of at least one or more of the following support groups: parents, spouse, siblings, or friends, with parents being the most commonly reported support group. Further, most participants indicated that earning a postsecondary degree was not only a means to an end but *their own dream* and believed that postsecondary education is necessary for all to succeed in life in general, not only the workplace. In the same study, participants' responses indicated a perception that having "wasta" or connections in the workplace could help secure a good job. Participants indicated that even if "wasta" helped a person to get a job, better qualifications were needed to be able to keep the job or to be promoted. However, participants who lived in farther away from urban centers tended to have more faith in "wasta" as an employment enhancer.

Concerns have been raised about the gender imbalance in postsecondary education among male and female Emiratis. Without proper education of the UAE national males, more than half of the proceeding generation will be ill-equipped to assume their roles in developing their country and providing for themselves and their families in an evolving technology-rich economic environment (Ridge 2009). As mentioned earlier, the gender gap in postsecondary education is particularly challenging in the UAE where males are held legally and financially responsible for their families.

9.3.2 *Postsecondary Education Best Practices and Technology*

The post-secondary education sector employs mostly expatriate teaches, instructors, and professors in both public and private educational institutions at all levels. Therefore, the teacher base in UAE educational sector is constantly changing from year-to-year. Typically, the average teacher needs the first year of a 3-year contract to proceed up the steep learning curve associated with adjusting to expatriate life, the institutional culture, and the behaviors of their students. A certain number of teachers do not make the transition and leave after 1 year leaving gaps to be filled by new teachers who will need another year to acclimate (Daleure 2011).

Many teachers who are successful in the UAE context realize that one of the most important tools a teacher can employ is a genuine connection with the students. Studies show that in Arab countries, students' perceptions about their teachers affect their attitudes about their courses (Daleure 2010; Saafin2008). These attitudes can affect academic performance either positively or negatively. Educators are held in high esteem in the UAE and personal relationships are regarded as important not only in education but in business and in all spheres of life in the Gulf and Middle Eastern culture (Klein and Kuperman 2008).

To better prepare students to become lifelong learners, some educational institutions have recently employed techniques such as "flipping the classroom," a technique which allows students to preview prerecorded teacher input before class so that the higher order skills can be practiced during class time while the teacher is monitoring. Another enhancement is the stepped up use of learning management systems (LMS). In order to use the innovative teaching practices and educational technology including LMS effectively, the teachers must use class time to build the needed rapport with students and to link the importance of completing self-study materials or completing out of class assignments with success in the course and the needs of the workplace. Teachers must be initially trained and must update their skills regularly (Daleure 2010).

Educational technology including LMS is increasingly being used to supplement contact teacher time and create efficiencies. In the UAE context, specific challenges exist including students' general underdeveloped reading skills, students lack of general knowledge and part-time work experience, and underdeveloped soft skills including time-management and internal motivation. The key to overcoming these difficulties lies in the teacher. By cultivating the roles of learning facilitator, mentor, and guide rather than merely a disseminator of information, the teacher must use the valuable classroom time to link the importance of completing the out of class activities to being successful in the course and being able to be successful in the workplace.

Teachers in public post-secondary educational institutions are constantly trained or retrained to keep abreast of developments in educational technology trends and innovations. The training includes ways to motivate students, encourage students, and impassion students to not only participate in required work but also to seek out new learning opportunities to gain knowledge and experience. Out of class activities become boring and burdensome if perceived as merely busy work or if students do not see clearly the value added to their learning experience (Downer and Daleure 2015).

In the UAE context, the public postsecondary education institutions invest heavily to develop the young Emiratis so that they can be successful in the workplace. Each student failure not only affects the student and the family, it represents lost investment of the government in the development of the country's future.

9.3.3 Family Involvement in Postsecondary Education

While literature is sparse on issues regarding education in the UAE, family involvement in education has been identified as a prime factor for success in the other countries where abundant literature exists including the US, Europe, and Australia. Mapp and Henderson (2002) compiled 51 studies in their work *A New Wave of Evidence: The Impact of School, Family, and Community Connections on Student Achievement* discussing important aspects of family involvement as success factors for students in all levels of education.

Studies including Ho (2003) stressed the importance of parental involvement in education in developing self-esteem, confidence, and a sense of overall well-being. Epstein and Shelden (2002) discussed the importance of family involvement in assuring that students main good attendance, the most basic requisite for learning. Studies including Carney-Hall (2008) examined family involvement in college and university students finding that parents and families are increasingly becoming involved in their young adult students' education. As educational costs rise in most developed and developing countries, necessitating the assistance of parents to help young adults cover the costs of a postsecondary education, parents feel more entitled to exert their opinions and engage in monitoring activities to assure good attendance and acceptable outcomes.

One of the few studies available in the UAE postsecondary educational context (Daleure et al. 2015) investigated links between family involvement and student success among Emirati students in federally funded postsecondary institutions. Selected results are presented in Tables 9.1 and 9.2.

Although not generalizable to all Emirati families, the study provides clues to understanding the complexities of postsecondary education in the UAE and its links to Emirati young adult unemployment. Daleure et al. (2015) found that although

Table 9.1 Study constructs indicating family support for postsecondary educational persistence (Daleure et al. 2015)

Q#	(Agree/strongly agree or always/most of the time)	Percentage (%)
Q56	My family encouraged me to go to college	97
Q49	My family provides money for food every day	95
Q36	My family provides the computer, printer, paper, and other tools I need to study	92
Q52	My family is very interested in my academic progress	91
Q48	My family insists that I respect my teachers and follow the college rules	88
Q40	My family stresses the importance of good grades	84
Q37	My family ensures that I am at college in time for my classes	82
Q29	My family is complimentary when I get good grades	76
Q34	I tell my family when I have a project, paper, or test to prepare for	67
Q45	My family encourages me to speak to my teacher, counselor, or supervisor when I have a problem at college	62

Table 9.2 Constructs indicating family not fully aware of behaviors needed for academic success (Daleure et al. 2015)

Q#	(Agree/strongly agree or always/most of the time)	Percentage (%)
Q65	I would do better if I had more support from my family	68
Q47	My family shows disapproval if I miss college when I am not ill	62
Q30	My family shows disapproval if I get bad grades	53
Q41	My family tries to limit the amount of time that I can visit with friends when I have college the next day	52
Q38	My family encourages me to get enough rest to be alert in college each day	49
Q33	My family checks to see that I have done my homework and other academic tasks	33
Q44	My family supports my participation in college clubs, activities, or sports	29
Q46	My family hires a tutor to help me with my college work	15
Q35	Someone in my family will quiz me to help me study before a test	10

families were supportive of their students' education shown in Table 9.1, family elders may not be fully aware of the commitment of time and effort needed for high academic achievement. Table 9.2 shows that no more than half the families were engaged in monitoring or supporting behaviors that are associated with developing effective study skills (Q30, Q41, Q38, Q33, Q44, Q46, Q35) and most students (68 %) indicated that they would do better if they had more support from their families.

In the same study, half the students had parents with primary or less education (father 50 %, mother 51 %) and only about one-fifth of the students had parents with more than a high school education (21 % fathers, 19 % mothers). Federally funded postsecondary institutions conduct courses in English while the students' native language is Arabic. However, only 22 % of the participants used English outside their educational institutions and only 9 % used English with their family and close friends.

The results of the study in no way imply neglect on the part of the parents or families, but rather highlight that the rate of rapid development outpaced the ability of society to keep up. As discussed earlier in this chapter, a formal education system did not exist at nationalization in 1971. That means that children who started in the first public school cohorts in around 1973 and continued on until graduation would have graduated in about 1985 at a time when finding a good paying job did not need a college education. At the same time, roughly the same cohort would be the youngest parents of today's college and university students.

Combining the parental education data, the English usage data, and the students' perceptions of family support, Daleure et al. (2014) concluded that many of the postsecondary students faced vastly different educational and social circumstances than their parents and elders experienced, yet the members of the younger generation were highly influenced by the well-meaning advice and opinions of their family elders.

> Coming from different economic environments, family elders may influence students to make program study choices in areas that do not match their skills and aptitudes in order to gain a credential perceived to be valuable for public sector employment which has become saturated. In addition, students believed that family members would find jobs for them even though measures are being taken to root out poor hiring practices such as nepotism, or hiring based on family influence, known as "wasta" in the UAE (Daleure et al. 2014, p. 24).

Maintaining the fine line between cultivating and utilizing business contacts and engaging in unethical business practices is something that organizations and companies all over the globe struggle to achieve. *Wasta* can be defined as "the utilization and employment of personal connections that give people advantages that they would otherwise not merit, thereby creating an unjust and efficient allocation of funds, services and/or positions" (Kropf and Newberry-Smith 2016, p. 3).

A study examining the business practices characterized as "wasta" using the World Bank Governance Indicators rated the UAE as 26 (lower ranking indicating less wasta in business practices) just below Austria. In the same study Kuwait was ranked 69 one rank below Italy at 70. The study found that the UAE and Qatar have "approached the ranks obtained by the USA, although they are still far away from the Scandinavian states" in terms of rankings (Ramady 2016. p. ix). Any lingering behaviors seem to have a greater influence on hiring decisions among GCC nationals than on hiring decisions among expatriates in GCC countries.

Leadership skills, critical thinking skills, punctuality, high attendance, teamwork, and the ability to link learning to practice are considered as soft skills desired by private sector employers according to studies including Alshaiba (2014).

According to Al-Ali (2013), Behery (2009), Shallal (2011), Sherif (2013), and Toledo (2013), Emiratis often lack soft skills, a major complaint from private sector employers, the origin of which may have its roots in the home environment. Low family support for students to participate in college clubs, activities, or sports (only 29 %) explains why most students (81 %) do not participate in extracurricular activities. Families provide all financial and logistical support for most students without which students are not be able to pay fees, buy uniforms, remain behind at college after regular hours, travel to competitions, and do other activities. The demonstrated low family support for extracurricular activities combined with low student participation rates suggest that students are not encouraged to develop the soft skills necessary to be successful in the rapidly changing modern workplace (Daleure et al. 2015).

Studies, including Ridge (2010), found that there is a general lack of career preparation prior to entering postsecondary education programs. Students often choose study programs according to advice from family members which may be based on perceptions about jobs with high salaries or quick promotions, not based on which programs suit the skills and aptitudes of the students and lead to jobs fostering internal fulfillment. With little affinity to the chosen program of study, and with little support in developing good study habits, students depend on the teacher to provide the motivating role in the classroom and dictate required learning activities for in class and outside of class activities. Students have not been trained in high school to seek out independent learning activities to augment in class activities which have not been assigned by the teacher (Wagie and Fox 2006).

Studies (Ridge 2009, 2010; Wagie and Fox 2005; Zuraik 2005) have shown that in the relatively young public education system in the UAE, primary, and secondary school students who are now college-agers have been exposed to largely rote methods of instruction, teachers who focus on getting through ministry approved curricula rather than fostering a love of learning, and reward repetition rather than intellectual curiosity.

Emirati college students often choose to study areas that do not match their skill sets and aptitudes to gain credentials perceived to be valuable in public sector employment so they can be like their parents (Ahmad 2011). In the Family Involvement Study, 72 % of the students in the study believed that their family would find them jobs when they graduate and 64 % reported that their families influenced their program decision. There is a clear tendency for the members of the older generations, who had enjoyed favorable working conditions of the public sector, to counsel their young adults to go into the public sector without realizing how much the job market has changed in recent years. The issue has become so important that the Gulf Cooperation Council (GCC) countries have recently been implementing measures to root out poor hiring practices based on family influence (Al-Ali 2013). If families continue to actively encourage young Emiratis—especially females who need parental or spousal permission to work to seek only public sector positions, little can be done by educational institutions or policymakers to increase private sector employment.

Issues such as those raised in the preceding paragraphs were addressed in *The Arab Knowledge Report* 2010/2011*: Preparing Future Generations for the Knowledge Society* (United Nations Development Programme/Regional Bureau for Arab States and Mohamed bin Rashid Al Maktoum Foundation 2011). The report found that the educational issues needing the most attention to prepare Emiratis for the knowledge economy were early education, English literacy, and the developing and awareness of how to address social and cultural factors present in the workplace. The report advocated for increased family involvement to assist in achieving educational aims and addressing social and cultural factors.

Ridge's (2010) study supported the argument that parents must be more active in their students' education by "demanding higher standards from their [male] students" (p. 29) because "Arab societies emphasize the authority of the parents, especially the fathers" (Wagie and Fox 2005, p. 284). Schools, according to Ridge (2010), faced "a lack of support from parents, often around disciplinary matters" (p. 29) and did not engage in regular communication with parents regarding student progress and achievement. Ridge added that parents who had little or no formal education tended to expect male students to work as early as possible rather than to pursue education beyond compulsory levels.

Classic studies from the United States (Eagle 1989; Henderson and Mapp 2002; Howland et al. 2006) support the findings of *Arab Knowledge Report* (2011) and Daleure et al. (2014) emphasizing the findings about family involvement that are similar to the UAE context and the context of the United States (US):

- mother's education level with higher educational levels linked to better student academic performance
- father's education level with higher educational levels linked to better student academic performance
- father's occupation and/or retirement with students in the UAE of retired fathers more likely to have low academic performance.

Factors for low academic performance that pertain to the UAE context include the following:

- Larger families with more extended family members living in the same households.
- Parents who did not complete high school.
- First language other than English used in the home (supported by Engstrom and Tinto 2008).
- Financial constraints and lack of parental support for education.
- Pressure for young people, particularly males, to work during school years, not pursue higher education, or even drop out of high school before completing.
- Low emphasis or indifference toward education for females assuming that females would be married to males who would provide for them.

In the abundant literature available on Western contexts, the family involvement behaviors and home environment factors mentioned in this section are consistently linked to academic performance at all levels of education (Henderson and Mapp 2002; Howland et al. 2006). However, sparse academic literature exists on the effects of family involvement of students in the UAE. Understanding the relationships among home environment, family involvement behaviors, and academic performance in the UAE represents a dimension of insight critical to establishing effective educational policies to increase student retention and achievement and better prepare for students for future employment (Daleure et al. 2015).

As previously mentioned, the *Ministry of Education Strategy 2010–2020* document (Government of the UAE 2010) has taken the issues mentioned on board and initiated the process for upgrading the educational system. One very important aspect of the strategy is including parents and the community in the process as advocated by the studies presented in this subsection and as described in more detail in the next subsection.

9.4 Progress Toward Educational Goals

Education is seen a high priority in the UAE so addressing the educational needs, i.e., improving the educational system of the UAE has been given increased attention in recent years. At all levels from KG to universities to up to the ministerial levels, changes have occurred to improve the education and employability of the country's most important resources, its human resources. The following is a brief overview of selected points targeted to enhance the educational system and better prepare Emirati youth for success in the workplace.

As previously mentioned Emirati males from 18 and 30 years old must attend compulsory military service of 12 months for high school completers and 2 years for those who did not complete high school. A recent program was announced for Emirati males aged 30–40 years old to volunteer for military service. During military service, the young men learn technical skills related to protecting the nation and develop soft skills including discipline, motivation, ability to work under stress, teamwork, and other essential life skills (UAE extends national 2016).

In 2014, signaled by the appointment of a new Vice Chancellor, the Higher Colleges of Technology, the country's largest postsecondary educator of Emiratis, entered a period of upgrade called HCT 2.0, conceptualized to focus even more on the needs of the workplace and geared to make graduates even more employable than before. A slight change in admission criteria occurred enabling students who had been through the admissions system to leave the system (i.e., attend military service, gain work experience, stay home for a couple semesters with an new baby, etc.) then return to complete a degree at a later stage. Previously only fresh high school leavers were eligible to attend federally funded educational institutions. This added flexibility allows fresh graduates to get work experience then return either full or part-time to continue their studies (HCT continues transformational 2016).

Changing communication styles have contributed to a shift in educational program offerings, requirements, and pedagogy in the nationals federally funded institutions to further enhance employability of Emirati graduates. A study by Allagui and Breslow (2011) found that 67 % the 18 year old Emiratis surveyed indicated they spent more time using social media than interacting with teachers and family members. Widespread use of English language social media has raised concerns over deterioration of Arabic language proficiency among youth. An increased use of Arabeezi, Emirati spoken dialect of Arabic language written in social medial sites using English letters, is even more problematic. From 2013, two courses delivered in Arabic were added to the general requirements of all students in federally funded institutions.

The emirate of Abu Dhabi included education reform in its list of priorities related to economic development and efforts to evolve as an educational hub for the UAE and the region. The educational reforms include:

- Reducing the role of government in the direct provision of educational services
- Enabling a strengthened private sector to deliver more educational services on behalf of government
- Shifting the focus of government to that of regulator and supervisor of an education system with newly created standards matching world's best educational practice.
- Facilitating the increased participation of Emiratis in education administration and teaching
- Achieving cost efficiencies through new practices in the management of individual schools and new administrative structures for learning institutions across the emirate. (adapted from Government of Abu Dhabi 2007, p. 28)

To achieve these goals, the Abu Dhabi Education Council (ADEC), oversees education delivery in the Abu Dhabi including the city of Abu Dhabi, Al Ain, and the Western Region.

9.5 Remaining Challenges in Education

Integrating creativity and innovation into the curriculum at all levels of education is one goal of the curriculum reform that is taking place, however, to achieve this goal a paradigm shift must occur in the way teaching and learning is conceptualized and implemented (Yamin 2014). To identify and address the issues in education educators and policy makers must strike a delicate balance between "balancing the preservation of the Arabic mother tongue, the Islamic foundations of the country and the needs of the twenty-first century" especially when many of the experts hired to develop the curriculum share neither the Arabic language nor the Islamic traditions (Cordingly 2014, p. 66).

Alshaiba (2014) points out that higher education must not be viewed only as imparting technical skills. Higher education must also produce workers that have the soft skills needed to function in the global knowledge economy. Graduates must be equipped to function as agents of social progress able and ready to contribute to the development of their country, and at the same time, contribute to the economy by filling a demand in the labor market.

However, as shown in multiple studies by TANMIA, an organization run by the Ministry of Labor, Emiratis seeking jobs do not appear to have the skills that employers are seeking. TANMIA concluded that there was a mismatch between outcomes of the higher education system and the requirements of employers.

This mismatch occurred because a constructive and appropriate relationships between higher education and the labor market do not exist. Therefore, the connections between educational institutions and the labor market must be further strengthened and expanded to assure that the programs on offer and the skills gain by young Emirati graduates are desirable not only the current labor market but for the jobs of the future.

References

Ahmad, A. (2011, May 9). Pupils opt for wrong subjects. *The National Newspaper*, p. 4.

Al-Abed, I., Vine, P., Hellyer, P., & Vine, P. (Eds.). (2008). *United Arab Emirates Yearbook: 2008*. London: Trident Press.

Al-Ali, J. (2013). *Localizing the GCC workforce: A study and a manual for employers, employees, and job seekers*. Dubai: Masar Printing and Publishing.

Al-Sayegh, F. (1998). Merchant's role in a changing society: the case of Dubai, 1900–90. *Middle East Studies, 34*(1), 87–102.

Al-Sayegh, F. (2012). Women of the Gulf during the first half of the twentieth century: A comparative study of American missionary archives and local memory. In A. E. Sonbol (Ed.), *Gulf Women* (pp. 241–276). Qatar: Bloomsbury Qatar Foundation Publishing.

Allagui, I., & Breslow, H. (2011). The internet, fixity, and flow: Challenges to the articulation of an imagined community. In R. Fisher & D. Riha (Eds.), *New media and the politics of online communities*. Oxford: Inter-Disciplinary Press.

Alshaiba, A. (2014*). Key perspectives on preparing UAE nationals for employment. In The future of eduation in the UAE: Innovation and Knowledge production* (pp. 67–95). Abu Dhabi: The Emirates Center for Strategic Studies and Research (ECSSR).

Arab Knowledge Report. (2010/2011). Preparing future generations for the knowledge society. Dubai: Mohammed Bin Rashid Al Maktoum Foundation (MBRF) and The United Nations Development Programme/Regional Bureau for Arab States (UNDP/RBAS).

Behery, M. H. (2009). Person/organization job-fitting and affective commitment to the organization: Perspectives from the UAE. *Cross Cultural Management: An International Journal, 16*(2), 179–196.

Carney-Hall, K. C. (2008, Summer). Understanding current trends in family involvement. Chapter in book New Directions for Student Services. No. 122, pp. 3–14. Wiley Periodicals. doi:10.1002/ss.271

Cordingly, P. (2014). *Innovative school and curriculum design. In The Future of Education in the UAE: Innovation & Knowledge Production* (pp. 40–66). Abu Dhabi: The Emirates Center for Strategic Studies & Research (ECSSR).

Daleure, G. (2005). Reflections of post-secondary educational experiences of selected women of the United Arab Emirates (UAE): A qualitative investigation of the motivations, supports, rewards, and challenges of seven Emirati women in the year 2004. Doctoral dissertation: Ball State University. Available at http://eric.ed.gov/?q=daleure

Daleure, G. (2010). Harnessing students' perceptions of effective teachers in the United Arab Emirates (UAE) to promote more effective learning. *Annual Edition Journal of Accreditation Council for Business Schools and Programs (ACBSP), 1*(1), 83–90.

Daleure, G. (2011, November). Maximizing the effectiveness of classroom teaching with second language business students: The power punch of blended learning. *International Council for Business Schools and Programs (ACBSP) Annual Conference Proceedings, 1*(3), 376–386

Daleure, G., Abon, R., Hinkson, K., Ajaif, T., & McKeown, J. (2015). Family involvement in Emirati college student education and linkages to high and low achievement in the context of the United Arab Emirates. *Forum for International Research in Education (FIRE) Journal, 1* (3), 9–32.

Daleure, G., Kane, P., Abdalla, H., Rashid, M., Alaskar, S., Ibrahim, M., Anwar, M. et al. (2014). Using "holistic sustainability" to preserve unique cultural identity while participating in the contemporary global economic and social environment: the case of the United Arab Emirates. *Proceedings of the 4th Annual Leadership in Learning in the Asian Century conference.* Penang, Malaysia: ELLTA society.

Downer, A., & Daleure, G. M. (2015, May). *Acquiring Academic Reading and Writing Skills through Learning by Doing Activities and Flipped Classroom Lessons. Proceedings of the colloquium on english language teaching.* Sharjah, UAE: Sharjah University.

Eagle, E. (1989). *Socioeconomic status, family structure, and parental involvement: The correlates of achievement.* Berkeley, CA: U.S. Department of Education, American Education Research Association.

El-Saadi, H. (2012). Women and the economy: Pre-oil gulf states, 147–166. In Sonbol, A. E., (Ed.). Gulf women. Doha: Bloomsbury Qatar Foundation Publishing.

Engstrom, C. and Tinto, V. (2008). Access without support is not opportunity. *Change, 46.*

Epstein, J. and Sheldon, S. (2002, May/June). Present and accounted for: Inproving student attendance through family and community involvement. *The Journal of Education Research, 95*(5), 308–318.

Government of Abu Dhabi. (2007). *Policy agenda 2007–2008: The Emirate of Abu Dhabi.* Abu Dhabi, UAE: The Executive Council of Abu Dhabi.

Government of the UAE. (2010). *Ministry of Education Strategy 2010–2020.* Available at https://www.moe.gov.ae/Arabic/Docs/MOE%20_Strategy.pdf

HCT Continues Transformational Journey Towards Version 2.0 at Spring Conference. (2016). HCT News on Social Media. Available at http://news.hct.ac.ae/en/2016/02/hct-continues-transformational-journey-towards-version-2-0-spring-conference/

Henderson, A. T., & Mapp K. L. (2002). *A new wave of evidence: the impact of school, family, and community connections on student achievement. Annual Synthesis 2002.* Austin, TX: National Center for Family and community connections with schools.

Ho, E. S. (2003). Students' self-esteem in an Asian educational system: Contribution of parental family involvement and parental involvement. *School Community Journal, 13*(1), 65–79.

Howland, A., Anderson, J. A., Smiley, A. D., & Abbott, D. J. (2006). School liaisons: Bridging the gap between home and school. *School Community Journal, 16*(2), 47.

Kapur, V. (2016, February 8). Mohamed announces "biggest structural changes' to UAE government. Emirates 24/7 Newspaper Online. Available at http://www.emirates247.com/news/mohammed-announces-biggest-structural-changes-to-uae-government-2016-02-08-1.620129

Klein, H. A., & Kuperman, G. (2008). Through an Arab cultural lens. *Military Review, 88*(3), 88–102.

Klomgah, R. Y. (2007). Predictors of academic performance of university students: an application of the goal efficacy model. *College Student Journal, 41*(2), 407.

Kropf, A., & Newberry-Smith, T. C. (2016). Wasta as a form of social capital?: An international perspective. In Ramady, M.A. (Ed.), *The political economy of Wasta: Use and abuse of social capital networking*, (pp. vii–xxx). Switzerland: Springer International Publishing.

Mapp, K., & Henderson, A. T. (2002). *Annual Synthesis 2002: A new wave of evidence: The impact of school, family, and community connections on student achievement*. SEDL Texas: National Center for Family and Community Connections with Schools.

Ramady, M. A. (2016). Overview. In Ramady, M.A. (Ed.), *The political economy of Wasta: Use and abuse of social capital networking*, (pp. vii–xxx). Switzerland: Springer International Publishing.

Rensimer, L. (2015). *International and commercial education in Ras Al Khaimah: Policies, problem areas, and promise*. Policy paper no. 14. Ras Al Khaimah, UAE: Sheikh Saud bin Saqr Al Qasimi Foundation for Policy Research.

Ridge, N. (2009). The hidden gender gap in education in the UAE. Policy Brief no 6. Dubai: Dubai School of Government.

Ridge, N. (2010, May). *Teacher quality, gender, and nationality in the United Arab Emirates: A crisis for boys*. Working Paper Series 10-06, Dubai School of Government, Dubai.

Saafin, S. (2008). Arab tertiary students' perceptions of effective teachers. *Learning and teaching in higher education: Gulf Perspectives, 5*(2), 1–11.

Shallal, M. (2011). Job satisfaction among women in the United Arab Emirates. *Journal of International Women's Studies, 12*(3), 114–134.

Sherif, S. (2013). Macroeconomic policy, localization, and reducing unemployment: The crucial human resource issues for the UAE. *Competitiveness Review: An International Business Journal, 23*(2), 158–174.

Swan, M. (2010, September 21). Men break gender barrier at Zayed University's campus in Dubai. *The National Newspaper Online*. Available at http://www.thenational.ae/news/uae-news/education/men-break-gender-barrier-at-zayed-universitys-campus-in-dubai

Toledo, H. (2013). The political economy of emiratization in the UAE. *Journal of Economic Studies., 40*(1), 39–53.

UAE extends national military service extended to 12 months. (2016, March 8). *UAE Interact Website* available at http://www.uaeinteract.com/docs/UAE_extends_national_military_service_extended_to_12_months/74397.htm

Wagie, D., & Fox, W. (2005/2006). Transforming education in the UAE: Contributing to social progress and the new economy. *International Journal of Learning, 12*(7).

Yamin, T. S. (2014). *Excellence, creativity, and innovation in education. In the future of education in the UAE: Innovation & knowledge production* (pp. 13–39). Abu Dhabi: The Emirates Center for Strategic Studies & Research (ECSSR).

Zuraik, E. (2005). A study of success and failure patterns in the public high schools of the Emirate of Sharjah in the UAE. UNESCO Report. Sharjah, UAE; UNESCO. (Arabic and English)

Chapter 10
Emiratization Progress and Challenges

Abstract As shown in the previous chapters, in the early years of nationalization, imported labor provided the skilled and unskilled labor needed to grow and prosper. Expatriate workers were attracted from their own countries by the salaries and working conditions offered in the UAE which were perceived as preferable to salaries and working conditions in their home countries. Expatriate workers remit substantial portions of their salaries to their own countries, thereby, removing the funds from the UAE local economy while supplementing the economic activities of their home countries. Expatriate workers are often provided in-kind supplements to salary that effectively reduce their cost of living including but not limited to free transport by company transport vehicle, free or low cost food prepared by company food service entities, free or low cost accommodation, reduced prices for retail products such as clothing, beauty products, or services that are provided by the employer to customers for sale. In the past half century, the basic infrastructure of the county has been established, two full generations have passed through secondary school in the educational system with more than a third progressing on to tertiary education, health care is available to all citizens, and the standard of living is among the highest in the world. Yet to achieve sustainable growth, the UAE must assure that young Emirati adults be able to find jobs that support the cost of living as it has evolved.

Keywords Emiratization · UAE labor market · UAE work force

10.1 Underlying Dichotomy of Sustainability Versus Complementarity of Labor

As shown in the previous chapters, in the early years of nationalization, imported labor provided the skilled and unskilled labor needed to grow and prosper. In the past half century, the basic infrastructure of the county has been established, two full generations have passed through secondary school in the educational system with more than a third progressing on to tertiary education, health care is available

G. Daleure, *Emiratization in the UAE Labor Market*,
DOI 10.1007/978-981-10-2765-9_10

to all citizens, and the standard of living is among the highest in the world. Yet to achieve sustainable growth, the UAE must assure that young Emirati adults are able to secure jobs that support the cost of living as it has evolved in the UAE.

Experts including Toledo (2006) highlight the dichotomy of the UAE labor market in terms of *sustainability versus complementarity* of labor. This means that for the economy to be sustainable and competitive, UAE nationals must be able to find jobs that can support the cost of living in the UAE context. However, as shown in previous chapters, stiff competition exists between Emiratis and expatriates for the desirable jobs.

As previously discussed, most (up to 80 %) of the jobs available in the UAE are jobs that offer salaries that are below the cost of living in the Emirati context. *Complementarity,* as discussed by Toledo (2006), and supported by Forestenlechner and Mellah (2011) refers to hiring enough skilled non-national workers at a sub-standard wage to balance out hiring Emiratis at a wage that is perceived suitable to them. In other words the *reservation wage*—actual wage that Emiratis will work for—is higher than the wage offered by private sector employers and being held artificially high by the *competition wage*—perceived wage available in the public sector. A re-aligning of salaries and perceptions of acceptible salaries, according to some experts, must be done to assure that labor costs do not rise so high that companies relocate to reduce labor costs and thereby remove jobs from the economy.

To experts who focus almost exclusively on the labor demand and supply theorems to explain the UAE labor market, the solution to full Emirati employment is to have Emiratis accept salaries and working conditions that do not meet their expectations. Their assumption is that because foreign labor is abundantly available and affordable, Emirati employees should adjust their own salary expectations to be closer to the salary expectations of foreign workers (Zimmerman 2015). This logic, however, does not take into account the spending patterns of UAE nationals and expatriate workers and the GDP losses in remittances as explained in the preceeding chapters.

10.2 Costs and Benefits of Emirati and Expatriate Employees

The costs and benefits considerations behind hiring decisions for Emirati and expatriate employees remain a hotly debated topic in the press and in academic publications (Sidani and Thornberry 2010). Some experts consider that the cost of employing Emirati employees is so prohibitively high that if required to hire more Emiratis, foreign companies would rather relocate (Toledo 2006). Other experts maintain that companies who prefer to hire lower cost expatriate employees do so only to take advantage of the incentives offered by the leadership to foreign companies while side-stepping labor policies of their own countries (Willoughby 2005). This section aims to present the varying opinions of these experts and others to construct a comprehensive view of the issues surrounding the success (or lack of success) of Emiratization practices.

Expatriate workers were attracted from their own countries by the salaries and working conditions offered in the UAE which were perceived as preferable to salaries and working conditions in their home countries (Yousef 2005). Expatriate workers remit substantial portions of their salaries to their own countries, thereby, removing the funds from the UAE domestic economy while supplementing the economic activities of their home countries (Naidu et al. 2014). Expatriate workers are often provided in-kind supplements to salary that effectively reduce their cost of living, often including, but not limited to free transport by company transport vehicle, free or low cost food prepared by company food service entities, free or low cost accommodation, trip tickets to their home country annually or bi-annually, tuition assistance for their children in private schools, reduced prices for retail products such as clothing, beauty products, or services that are provided by the employer to customers for sale.

The salary expectations for Emirati employees may be higher than migrant employees but Emiratis spend nearly all their salaries on products and services inside the country thereby adding to the overall GDP of the country. More new Emirati entrants to the workforce have a postsecondary education and English communication skills (Sherif 2013). Companies who employ Emiratis do not have to pay for employment visas, initial and final trip tickets, or fees to labor offices which contain hefty taxes to home country governments. Emiratis provide for their own transport and accommodation. Therefore, the higher salary expectations of the Emirati employees is offset at least partially by the savings of the costs and expenses mentioned in this section.

Recent changes in labor laws allow foreign workers to change jobs provided they give proper notice allowing more flexibility and lowering costs for employers. Some experts, including Zimmerman (2015) advocate more flexibility in the labor market as a way to increase productivity with the returns on productivity offsetting the higher wages paid to Emirati employees.

10.3 A Look Toward the Future

As demonstrated in the preceding chapters, foreign labor at first filled gaps in the labor market that could not be filled with the small Emirati population and provided quick expertise while the nation took the time to educate and prepare its people. The influx of foreign labor provided the added benefit of a sizeable consumer market to further accelerate economic growth. The economy of the UAE weathered the financial downturn of 2008 and has remained stable even as oil prices plummeted in the mid-2010s. However, especially in the face of decreasing oil prices, unemployed Emiratis must enter the workforce. The methods that the government of the UAE has used over the years are described in this subsection.

At the federal level an organization called TANMIA, part of the Ministry of Labor, has been charged with "generation of job opportunities for the UAE national workforce, a reduction in unemployment, the improvement of skills and productivity of the national workforce, and the proposal of appropriate policies to the federal government to improve the implementation of Emiratization" Alshaiba (2014).

Emiratization, according to experts including Behery (2009), must not be carried out as if the goal is to merely substitute Emiratis for foreign workers. The goal of Emiratization efforts is to employ Emiratis desiring to work in jobs that are suited to their skills, abilities, and aptitudes with the Emiratis being considered as the employees of choice due to their productivity and the advantages associated with hiring citizen employees. Therefore, Emiratization must be conceptualized as more closely assigning the skills and abilities of the Emirati job seekers with the needs of the private sector employers, while at the same time, aligning the expectations of the Emirati job seekers in terms of salaries, benefits, and working conditions more closely to those offered by private sector employers (Al-Ali 2013).

The *UAE Vision 2021* (2010) document emphasizes that economic sustainability cannot be achieved in isolation of cultural, environmental, and social sustainability exemplifying the holistic sustainability model advocated by Sharma and Ruud (2003) and Warburton (2003). Holistically sustainable practices encompassing economic, social, cultural, and political must be integrated in the corporate environment and be promoted at all levels of the education system for sustainable development to take place.

The complexity of the issues associated with Emirati unemployment, especially high unemployment among educated young Emirati adults, and Emiratization efforts, are being tackled by the leadership of the country in creative and innovative ways.

As shown in the preceding chapters, the UAE is well positioned for economic success going into the future if sustainable employment of Emirati can be achieved. New labor policies that increase flexibility in the labor market for both Emiratis and expat workers, according to experts including Naidu et al. (2014) steps on the path toward more sustainable employment practices. Support for Naidu et al. (2014) can be seen in the *Employment and Salary Trends in the Gulf 2016* publication which states that

> UAE continues to dominate as the most attractive destination in the GCC for expatriates. 63 % of the professionals surveyed picked UAE as the place they would be most likely to move to. The country also enjoys the highest retention rate in the region with 88 % of expatriates already residing in the country expressing a desire to remain there (Gulf Talent 2016, p. 5).

The policy shift to allow greater mobility for expatriate employees, if utilized properly, may well serve goals of Emiratization, enrich the UAE labor market, and enhance the UAE economy (Zimmerman 2015). The following points support this concept of recycling expatriate expertise as a way to increase Emiratization effectiveness and encourage more spending and investment in the country.

Previous chapters identified and described important points including:

1. About 80 % of the jobs available in the private sector require only basic education and offer salaries that could not meet the needs of an Emirati family in the UAE.
2. Expatriate workers choose to come to the UAE because they find salaries, or working conditions, or living environment that they perceive as better than those available in the contexts of their home countries.
3. Expatriate workers are assured of basic living expenses through their employers including health care, accommodation, etc., either through direct provision or through allowances that supplement base salaries. In the case of the lowest paid workers, domestic workers, and laborers, employers provide accommodation, transport, and healthcare benefits and many provide even food.
4. Many expatriate employees send remittances to their home countries rather than investing in the UAE economy with some workers having their entire base salaries direct deposited to accounts in their home countries.
5. UAE nationals compete with expatriate labor who often possess higher qualifications and more experience and due to #2 are often willing to accept lower salaries that would otherwise be expected in the UAE labor market.
6. UAE nationals sometimes do not have the skills and/or experience desired by employer, especially in the private sector. Reasons could include inadequate preparation at primary, secondary, or tertiary educational institutions, mismatch in perceptions of skills that are needed in the workplace, or lack of proper guidance in career planning.
7. The leadership of the UAE is putting huge efforts into upgrading the curriculum, teaching staff, and facilities of public education at all levels including providing incentives to hire more Emirati teachers and administrators, and assuring that the program learning outcomes are aligned with the needs of the workplace, especially private sector employers.
8. Some Emirati employees avoid the private sector jobs because they perceive the salaries, benefits, or working conditions are not suitable. Emirati women, in particular, have found working under private sector conditions challenging when trying to maintain a home and work life balance.
9. Highly skilled expatriate professionals admitted on short-term (usually 3 year) renewable visas go through a steep learning curve when entering the UAE labor market. When highly skilled and experienced expatriates are replaced with less experienced UAE nationals during the Emiratization process, organizations may experience productivity losses.
10. Expatriates, experiencing fears of job insecurity, decrease spending in the UAE economy and increase remittances to their home countries, by-passing opportunities for investment in the local environment.

As stated at in the preface, this book attempts to describe and illustrate the issues contributing to Emirati unemployment, and the workings of the UAE labor market.

It will be up to the policymakers and future generations of Emiratis to work and come up with the solutions that integrate Emirati fresh graduates into the labor market, allow for Emiratis to advance through the ranks, enable Emiratis to embrace private sector job opportunities, and at the same time maximize the expatriate expertise that already resides in the country or will be hired to meet future needs.

Best wishes for success to the leadership and people of the UAE accompany this work. May they succeed in achieving the *UAE Vision 2021*.

References

Al-Ali, J. (2013). *Localizing the GCC workforce: A study and a manual for employers, employees, and job seekers*. Dubai: Masar Printing and Publishing.

Alshaiba, A. (2014). Key perspectives on preparing UAE nationals for employment. In *The future of education in the UAE: Innovation and Knowledge production* (pp. 67–95). Abu Dhabi: The Emirates Center for Strategic Studies and Research (ECSSR).

Behery, M. H. (2009). Person/organization job-fitting and affective commitment to the organization: Perspectives from the UAE. *Cross Cultural Management: An International Journal, 16*(2), 179–196.

Forestenlechner, I., & Mellah, K. (2011). Gaining legitimacy through hiring local workforce at a premium: The case of MNEs in the United Arab Emirates. *Journal of World Business*,. doi:10.1016/j.jwb.2010.10.006.

Government of the United Arab Emirates. (2009). *Employment, Wages, and Hours Worked Survey 2008*. Available at www.fcsa.gov.ae

Government of the UAE. (2010). *Vision 2021*. Abu Dhabi: Government of the UAE. Available at https://www.vision2021.ae/en

Gulf Talent. (2016, March). *Employment & Salary Trends in the Gulf*. Available at www.gulftalent.com

Naidu, S, Nyarko, Y., & Wang, S. Y. (2014, August). Worker Mobility in a global labor market: Evidence from the United Arab Emirates. *National Bureau of Economic Research (NBER) Working Paper No. 20388*. Cambridge, MA: National Bureau of Economic Research (NBER).

Sharma, S., & Ruud, A. (2003, August). On the path to sustainability: integrating social dimensions into research and practice of environmental management. *Business Strategy and Environment, Special Issue: Corporate Social Responsibility & Governance or Sustainability, 12*(4), 205–214.

Sherif, S. (2013). Macroeconomic policy, localization, and reducing unemployment: The crucial human resource issues for the UAE. *Competitiveness Review: An International Business Journal, 23*(2), 158–174.

Sidani, Y., & Thornberry, J. (2010). The current Arab world ethic: Antecedents, implications, and potential remedies. *Journal of Business Ethics, 91*(1), 35–49.

Toledo, H. (2006, January). *The problems and prospects of Emiratization: Immigration in an imperfect labor market*. Sharjah: American University Sharjah.

United Arab Emirates (UAE) Government. (2010). *United Arab Emirates Vision 2021*. Retrieved from http://www.vision2021.ae/downloads/UAE-Vision2021-Brochure-English.pdf

Warburton, K. (2003). Deep learning and education for sustainability. *International Journal of Sustainability in Higher Education, 4*(1), 44–56.

Willoughby, J. (2005, March). Ambivalent anxieties of the South Asian-Gulf Arab labor exchange. *Department of Economics Working Paper Series, No. 2005–02*. Washington, D.C.: American University. http://www.american.edu/cas/econ/workpap.htm

Yousef, T. (2005). The changing role of labor migration in Arab economic integration. *Policy seminar on Arab Economic Integration: Challenges and Prospects, February, 23–24, 2005.* Washington, D.C: Center for Contemporary Arab Studies.

Zimmerman, K. F. (2015). Circular migration. In K. F. Zimmerman & A. S. Kritikos (Eds.), *Evidence-based policy making in labor economics The IZA world of labor guide 2015*, (pp. 86–87). London: Bloomsbury.

Index

G. Daleure, *Emiratization in the UAE Labor Market*,
DOI 10.1007/978-981-10-2765-9

FSC
www.fsc.org
MIX
Papier | Fördert
gute Waldnutzung
FSC® C083411

Kolibri 360 GmbH
Ferdinand-Jühlke-Straße 7
99095 Erfurt, Deutschland
produktsicherheit@kolibri360.de